KitchenAid - The Food Processor Cookbook

THE FOOD PROCESSOR COOKBOOK

40 RECIPES AND HEALTHY-EATING TIPS FROM THREE EXPERTS

recipes by Veerle de Pooter | photography by Tony Le Duc

KitchenAid

ARTISAN   **KitchenAid**

THE FOOD PROCESSOR COOKBOOK
40 RECIPES AND HEALTHY-EATING TIPS FROM THREE EXPERTS

The KitchenAid Artisan 4L Food Processor produces professional results every time. It is powerful, reliable and versatile – slicing, chopping, grating, dicing and mixing accurately and efficiently.

The Food Processor features the revolutionary new ExactSlice system, which replicates even the most sophisticated knife skills. Cooks can adjust the slicing thickness instantaneously by simply sliding an external lever, without removing the blade or even turning the Food Processor off.

To illustrate the extraordinary results you can achieve with KitchenAid, Veerle de Pooter has worked with three experts – a nutritionist, a doctor and a chemist – to create 40 delicious new recipes.

These mouthwatering recipes are easy to reproduce, as many of them come with either step-by-step pictures or can be downloaded as a 'how-to' video. To watch one of the recipe videos, simply download the free Layar app onto your smartphone or tablet and scan the page containing the Layar icon: you will then immediately be redirected to the video.

This book also contains useful tips and advice from our three experts, including how to create tasty menus with good nutritional value, the healthy effects that fruit and vegetables have on our body and a closer look at foodpairing.

We hope that you will enjoy cooking these recipes for your friends and family and that it will inspire you to create your own using the KitchenAid Artisan 4L Food Processor.

Dirk Vermeiren
Managing Director KitchenAid Europa, Inc.

The interviewees As a doctor and nutritionist, Thierry Hanh has many years' experience in developing nutrionally balanced menus for chefs and clients. His theory that it is possible to love good food and eat well is borne out by the menus in this book. GP Marleen Finoulst believes we should all eat more fruit and vegetables. Make a start using our recipes. Bernard Lahousse and Peter Coucquyt are the pioneers of foodpairing, a tool which encourages the unexpected combination of ingredients. Use our recipes as inspiration to experiment with fruit and vegetables.

The master cutter The Artisan Food Processor is a master at cutting ingredients in different ways. Aside from the standard multifunctional blade – which also comes in a mini version – there are five different cutting functions. There's the 8 mm dicing kit, an innovation unique to the Artisan Food Processor, which chops ingredients into small cubes. Then there's the adjustable slicing disc, which allows you to control how thinly ingredients are sliced via an external lever. Separate discs for shredding vegetables, grating cheese and cutting fries complete the set.

The recipes Forty recipes put the healthy-eating advice from our experts into practice. They are grouped in such a way that each interview with an expert is immediately followed by a series of recipes, allowing you to see the interviewee's theory in practice. Throughout the book you will also find ten recipes in a step-by-step format, designed to guide you through the Artisan Food Processor's numerous functions.

The product range Potatoes, onions, tomatoes, root vegetables and citrus fruits are not only popular ingredients in European cooking, they are also ideally suited for use in the Artisan Food Processor. These five groups of fruits and vegetables are a thread throughout the book, regularly popping up in recipes – particularly the step-by-step sequences – and so providing a vitamin and mineral boost to their content.

The extras Some pages in this books have been enriched with Layar and contain digital content that you can view using your smartphone.

HOW IT WORKS:

Step 1: Download the free Layar app for iPhone or Android.

Step 2: Look for pages with the Layar logo.

Step 3: Open the Layar app, hold the phone above the page and tap to scan it.

Step 4: Hold your phone above the page to view the interactive content.

If you do not use LAYAR, you can watch the videos at: www.kitchenaid.eu/foodprocookbook.

Contents

Cutting techniques

BLADES

Multipurpose stainless steel blade

This is the most versatile blade of all and can be used for chopping, puréeing and mixing ingredients. It fits the work bowl with a very handy watertight seal, so that the blade can remain in the bowl while the contents are removed.

Mini multipurpose stainless steel blade

This smaller version of the multipurpose blade fits the mini-bowl and performs exactly the same functions but for smaller quantities.

Discs

Reversible shredding disc

The shredding disc is used for grating hard vegetables and fruits, for example carrots, potatoes or apples, as well as hard cheeses and even chocolate. The disc is reversible: just choose which side to use to produce fine or medium shreds. Use it in the work bowl or prep bowl to create delicious salads, röstis, bases for quiches and many more dishes in a flash.

Adjustable slicing disc

Thanks to the externally adjustable blade control, the slicing disc can produce anything from wafer-thin slivers to 5 mm thick slices. By applying more or less pressure while inserting the items through the feed tube, you can exercise even more control over the thickness of the slices. Be careful when handling this disc; use the finger holes provided to install it in either the work bowl or prep bowl.

Cutting techniques

DISCS

8 mm dicing kit

The dicing kit is useful for chopping vegetables and fruits, such as potatoes, onions, mangoes and melons, into 8 mm cubes. This kit is an innovation unique to the Artisan Food Processor and will allow you to create wonderful dishes, such as tartares, chunky soups, frittatas etc. Be careful when handling the items in the dicing kit, particularly the blade; use the finger holes provided to install the kit in either the work bowl or prep bowl.

French fry disc

This disc does exactly what it says on the tin; use it to cut potatoes or other firm vegetables into French fry shapes. Be careful when handling this disc; use the finger holes provided to install it in either the work bowl or prep bowl.

Grate/shave disc

The grate/shave disc is used for grating hard cheeses, such as Parmesan or Gruyère, crushing ice cubes for cocktails and shaving chocolate for desserts. Make sure that whenever you process cheese or chocolate, the ingredients are well chilled, otherwise you may end up with a sticky mess in the work bowl or prep bowl.

Peel 1 cucumber, 1 Spanish onion and 2 garlic cloves.

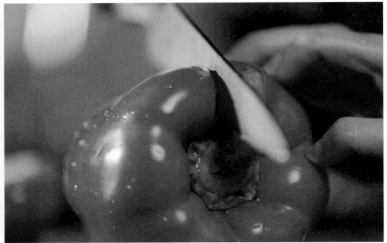

Deseed 2 red peppers. Roughly chop the prepared vegetables, plus 1 kg vine tomatoes. Purée all the vegetables with the multifunctional blade in the work bowl on speed 2.

Add 1 tbsp sweet paprika and 2 tbsp sherry vinegar. Process again. Add 150 ml extra virgin olive oil through the feed tube while the motor is running. Season with salt and pepper.

Chill for several hours, preferably overnight, to allow the flavours to develop. Meanwhile, finely chop 75 g ham, 3 large gherkins, 2 hard-boiled eggs and a few sprigs of flat-leaf parsley.

Dice 3 slices of bread and pan-fry until golden brown and crispy. Serve the gazpacho in chilled bowls, sprinkled with the garnishes and some extra virgin olive oil.

Tomatoes

TOMATO

- the tomato is one of the world's favourite vegetables, as shown by the popularity of the 'heritage' varieties now appearing in shops
- a ripe tomato is at its best eaten raw; slightly under-ripe they benefit from a little heat by stewing, roasting or grilling with a pinch of sugar to bring out the flavour
- tomatoes contain high levels of lycopene, an antioxidant thought to protect against prostate cancer

BLACK TOMATO

- black tomatoes are characterised by dark-brown to black skin, although the flesh is red with an earthy, almost smoky flavour
- one of the best-known black tomato varieties is Black Krim, so-called because it originated in Russia

GREEN TOMATO

- if you think green tomatoes are under-ripe, you are mistaken; some tomatoes remain a vibrant green colour even when ripe, eg Green Zebra or Evergreen
- green tomatoes tend to be less acidic than their red counterparts and are therefore ideal for use in jams, chutneys and even desserts

BEEFSTEAK TOMATO

- the beefsteak tomato is one of the largest varieties with individual fruits reaching up to 450 grams; varieties include Marmande and Ox Heart
- the sweet and juicy flesh of the beefsteak tomato makes it perfect for slicing into salads, sandwiches and carpaccios

PLUM TOMATO

• the plum tomato – one well-known variety is San Marzano – has an elongated shape and less juicy flesh than other varieties
• plum tomatoes are ideal for frying, baking, drying and puréeing into sauces but less good for eating raw

CHERRY TOMATO

• the term 'cherry' is something of a misnomer, since not all cherry tomatoes are round or red; some are yellow or orange and still others are pear-shaped (eg Yellow Pear)
• cherry tomatoes are often eaten raw as a snack or used in salads but they actually taste much better roasted when their natural sugars have had time to develop

WHITE TOMATO

• white tomatoes are part of the heritage varieties which are cropping up in our shops right now; examples are White Beauty and Great White
• the white tomato has the sweetest flavour of all tomatoes and therefore works well in sweet and savoury dishes (technically speaking, a tomato is a fruit and not a vegetable)

Onions

ONION
• onions have brown or yellow skin and creamy flesh which ranges from moderately to extremely pungent in flavour
• although onions are mostly used as the basis for many dishes, you can use them as a vegetable in their own right: they are great stuffed, roasted or puréed into soups
• onions contain potassium, vitamin C, folic acid and vitamin B6

GARLIC
• there are numerous varieties of garlic, from the small-cloved Rocambole to bulbs consisting of a single clove, ie Elephant Garlic
• garlic is thought to play a role in the prevention of coronary heart disease but you would have to eat at least 7 cloves a day to feel the effects!

SPRING ONION
• the flavour of spring onions ranges somewhere between ordinary onions and chives; use them raw in tomato or potato salads, or gently softened in butter with steamed green vegetables
• spring onions contain large amounts of vitamin C and A, potassium and iron

LEEK
• the leek has a refined sweet flavour which is best appreciated by serving the vegetable cooked, although you can eat leeks raw
• leeks are a perfect match for potatoes, eggs, cheese and ham in soups, gratins and quiches; or serve baby leeks roasted or steamed with a Mediterranean-style dressing
• leeks contain large amounts of folic acid, iron and potassium

RED ONION

• the red onion has attractive purple-and-white flesh with a crisp texture; the flavour ranges from sweet and mild to quite sharp

• red onions are delicious eaten raw in salads and salsas; they combine equally well with fruits, such as blood oranges and mangoes, or vegetables such as fennel or radicchio

SHALLOT

• the shallot has a distinctive aroma which is milder and sweeter than the onion; this makes it a favourite of chefs all around the world

• you can use shallots in the same way as onions but remember: you can substitute shallots for onions but not the other way around

• shallots contain twice the amount of vitamin C of onions

GREEN GARLIC

• green garlic – also called 'wet garlic' – is harvested before the plant has matured in early summer; the bulbs have soft, pliable skin with barely formed cloves

• because of its grassy sweet flavour, green garlic can be used raw in salads, dips and dressings

Potatoes

KING EDWARD
• the King Edward is an English potato variety which dates back to 1902; the oval-shaped tubers are characterised by pink blushes on the skin
• this is the ideal variety for crispy roast potatoes and fluffy mash

BINTJE
• the Bintje produces large tubers with fairly firm flesh and a neutral flavour, making it an excellent all-rounder, perfect for fries, salads, mash, röstis etc
• this variety was developed by a Dutch headmaster in 1905 and named after one of his former students

VITELOTTE
• the Vitelotte or 'truffle potato' is a bit of an outsider due to its striking purple skin and flesh
• purple potatoes are best roasted or steamed, as the colour tends to leach into the cooking liquid

CORNE DE GATTE
• the Corne de Gatte owes its name to its shape which resembles a goat's horns; the pinkish skin hides very firm flesh with a sweet, nutty flavour
• this variety is ideal for roasting or baking under a salt crust, two cooking methods which will intensify the flavour

Opperdoezer

• the Opperdoezer produces oval tubers with a very thin skin, creamy yellow flesh and waxy texture

• this variety can only be cultivated in the village of Opperdoes in northern Holland; it is valued as a delicacy because of its refined flavour

Jersey Royal

• the Jersey Royal has been grown on the island of Jersey for over 130 years and now enjoys a Protected Designation of Origin status

• Jersey Royals are highly prized for their unique flavour and texture, which is why they are usually enjoyed simply boiled or steamed with a little melted butter

Ratte

• the Ratte produces small, elongated tubers with a waxy texture and chestnut-like flavour

• make the most of the Ratte's sweet flavour by boiling or steaming the potatoes in their skins and then crushing them with butter or olive oil

Citrus

LIME

• limes produce a fragrant zest and juice; us[e] them in the same way you would lemons
• to make limes easier to squeeze, roll them under the palm of your hand: this breaks down the segments and releases the juice
• limes contain useful amounts of vitamin C

LEMON

• lemons are indispensable in the kitchen: their sour juice is a great substitute for salt as a seasoning and it prevents ingredients from oxidising, ie turning brown when exposed to the air
• lemon zest adds an extra dimension to salads, seafood dishes, creamy desserts, pastry etc.
• lemons contain large amounts of vitamin C, potassium and folic acid

ORANGE

• the orange is an extremely versatile fruit to cook with: their flavour ranges from honeysweet to quite tart and the zest can be used to flavour all kinds of dishes
• oranges are a great match for seafood, duck and pork, as well as root vegetables and orange-coloured fruit
• oranges contain large amounts of vitamin C and potassium

POMELO

• this giant member of the citrus family – also called 'shaddock' – can grow up to 25 cm in diameter and 2 kg in weight
• the pomelo has very thick skin and light green flesh with a mild, sweet flavour; the skin can be pickled or candied

MANDARIN

- the mandarin looks like a small, slightly flattened orange; the soft, sweet and fragrant flesh is easy to divide into segments
- mandarins contain large amounts of vitamin C

BLOOD ORANGE

- this orange hybrid with red-blushed skin and ruby flesh was first cultivated in 1850; the flavour can range from sweet-sour to quite acidic
- make the most of blood oranges by using the bright red juice in sorbets, vinaigrettes, custards and marinades
- blood oranges combine very well with fennel, chicory, feta, seafood and fish

GRAPEFRUIT

- the grapefruit has yellow, pink or red flesh which can be enjoyed by eating the fruit raw or by squeezing the juice
- the bittersweet flavour of grapefruit is delicious when grilled and combined with chicken, pork, seafood or avocado
- grapefruits contain large amounts of vitamins C and A and folic acid

Roots

RADISH

• radishes are the babies among root vegetables but do not let their small size and colourful appearance fool you, they can pack quite a punch

• radishes are mostly eaten raw in vinaigrettes, pickles, carpaccios, salsas etc, to go with smoked fish, cold meats and dairy produce

• do not forget to remove the tops as soon as you buy radishes, otherwise they will start to wilt and lose their crunchy texture

CARROT

• not all carrots are orange: they exist in all shapes, sizes and colours, for example the aptly-named Cosmic Purple or the conical-shaped Chantenay

• in terms of flavour, carrots are at their best roasted or cooked in a syrupy glaze; combine carrots with ingredients which emphasise or contrast their sweetness, such as lime, coriander, maple syrup and orange

• carrots contain large amounts of vitamin A, C, and B, folic acid and potassium

BEETROOT

• accentuate the earthy flavour of beetroot with the salty, pungent and bitter aromas of smoked fish, horseradish, rocket or radicchio

• when boiling beetroot leave the skin on, otherwise the juices will leach into the cooking water; or roast beetroot in the oven: this will allow the natural sugars to caramelise

• beetroot contains high levels of potassium, vitamins A and C and magnesium

CELERIAC

• celeriac's pock-marked skin hides extremely tasty and versatile flesh; eaten raw, it is delicious grated into salads with mustard, dill or horseradish cream

• when cooked celeriac tastes slightly sweet and nutty; perfect with roast pork, venison or wild boar, baked sweet potatoes and pumpkin

• celeriac contains vitamin C, potassium and phosphor

Parsnip

• the parsnip is an underrated vegetable: enjoy its sweet and nutty flavour by roasting it, this allows the natural sugars to develop
• parsnips love the company of honey, citrus, mustard, warm spices (cinnamon, ginger) and woody herbs (rosemary, sage), dairy products and pork
• whether you serve parsnips roasted, puréed or boiled, they will provide you with potassium, folic acid and vitamin C

Turnip

• the best-known variety of turnips has purplish-white skin and a delicate, slightly bitter taste; however, the sweetest variety (Golden Ball) is yellow and has an almost buttery flavour
• turnips are globetrotters, they crop up in every world cuisine and can therefore be combined with a wide range of flavours: coriander, orange, honey, cumin... even vanilla
• turnips are a great source of vitamin C

Sweet potato

• despite their name, sweet potatoes are actually root vegetables; some have juicy orange flesh, whereas white-fleshed sweet potatoes tend to be more mealy
• sweet potatoes can be prepared just like ordinary potatoes but their sweet taste makes them a great match for exotic flavours, such as lime, coconut, lemongrass, ginger and chilli
• sweet potatoes – particularly orange ones – contain large amounts of vitamin A and potassium

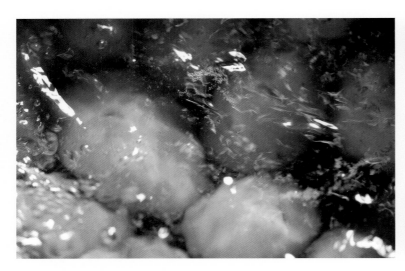

Boil 300 g waxy potatoes unpeeled for 10 minutes, then drain. Peel the potatoes when they are cool enough to handle and grate them with the reversible shredding disc, medium side up, in the prep bowl on speed 1.

Place in a bowl and add 400 g white crabmeat, 1 tbsp cumin seeds and 1 tsp harissa (Moroccan chilli paste). Finely chop ⅛ preserved lemon, ½ bunch of coriander and 4 spring onions. Add to the bowl, season and mix well.

Shape into 8 patties and chill for 1 hour. Slice 2 peeled and deseeded cucumbers with the adjustable slicing disc on the medium setting on speed 1.

Whisk together 2 tbsp white wine vinegar, 1 tbsp clear honey, ½ tsp harissa, 1 tbp poppy seeds and 4 tbsp olive oil. Finely chop ½ bunch of mint, add to the dressing and season with salt. Toss with the cucumber.

Pan-fry the crab rösti in vegetable oil on both sides until golden brown and crispy. Serve with the cucumber salad.

03 INTERVIEW WITH THE NUTRITIONIST

Treat yourself but keep your needs under control.

I have been a medical doctor and nutritionist for thirty years. I started working for the pharmaceutical industry as a medical director for a company in the business of manufacturing artificial nutrition for people unable to feed themselves. It involved a very specific type of nutrition which is administered intravenously. It is a very complex process to introduce fats into the veins and at the time only one laboratory in the world was able to do this. Things are different now because we understand the process better but then it was extremely important to produce small droplets of fat to ensure that they would disperse throughout the body without causing a fat embolism. So those were my first forays into the application of nutritional theory.

Before that, I had already got to know the science of nutrition through my work in medical reanimation. I did that for more or less ten years, after which I established a consultancy agency – HAT Consultants – with the aim of offering support on a scientific and nutritional level to businesses of varied backgrounds, such as pharmaceutical companies and thermal complexes (i.e. spas).

My work with chefs came about as a result of my interest in therapeutic prevention, which in turn was aroused by my collaboration with spas. At a spa a client's eating habits are reviewed. In other words: a dietician will prescribe a certain diet but the client must then be able to translate this 'prescription' for his own use. The same goes for the chefs at these spas: they must also be able translate these prescriptions. All of which gave rise to the idea of training chefs 'from prescription to plate'. This training is always a one-on-one affair between a nutritionist and a chef so that a maximum amount of knowledge can be transmitted, regarding the choice of ingredients, portion size, presentation on the plate etc – all this without losing out on flavour or pleasure of eating. The aim of this training is to develop skills which will allow chefs to create balanced menus, not individual dishes.

Dr Thierry Hanh is a medical doctor, nutritionist and consultant for the pharmaceutical industry. His mission is to teach chefs how to create balanced, healthy and nutritious menus which are also full of flavour.

Flavour, pleasure and health are key concepts in the charter I use as a guide for my training. Chefs who take the training will, at the end of it, be able to tranform this charter into balanced, nutritious and tasty menus. That is why I place so much emphasis on the skills of the nutritionist-chef duo. These skills range all the way from choice of primary ingredient to presentation on the plate. For example: to allow only 80 or 100 grams of meat per portion is totally unacceptable for most top chefs. But there are little tricks to present this amount differently: you can slice the meat thinner or arrange it in a fan shape on the plate. 80 or 100 grams may seem little but if you have a menu with a starter, a main course and a dessert, this amount of protein is actually enough.

In other words, generosity should no longer be the guideline for portion sizes, chefs should be guided by what their customers really need. These two things are not always the same. Many people go out to a restaurant because they want to eat well. That often means they expect a generous portion, they want value for money. But there is a minority of customers who are in the habit of eating out and who feel the need to eat just enough. People often decide to eat just one course because the portions are so generous. I think that restaurant owners are getting it wrong: if they were to serve smaller portions, customers would happily order more than one course. Customers would have no problems ordering a balanced menu – including starter, main course and dessert – over one single dish. This has several advantages. There is more nutritional variation in two or three courses than in one single dish. And because the courses are served one after the other, there is more time to digest each course. This means that you get to dessert much more relaxed and with a great deal of pleasure. On top of that, all this benefits chefs financially as well.

But I am not a stickler for detail, I do not measure everything to the last gram. As far as I am concerned, everybody is allowed everything. You have to allow yourself a treat now and again, a good roast with all the trimmings for example. It means you will pay more attention to what you eat before and after and so avoid an excess intake of calories. But it is important to keep your needs under control: you cannot fancy a treat morning, noon and night. In that respect it is important to make a distinction between gourmets and gluttons. Gluttony is just stuffing yourself, a gourmet is somebody who enjoys food. For the latter 50 or 100 grams is sufficient but for a glutton even 500 grams is not enough. I think it is a shame that a distinction is always made between pleasure and nutrition. Many top chefs seem to think that it is impossible to combine both.

The million-dollar question is: does food have a gender? Despite all the advances that have been made in the past decades, there can be no equality between men and women... as far as food is concerned. An adult woman is allowed 2,000 calories a day, a man 2,500. Why? Because a man's and a woman's bodies are totally different. A woman gives life, a man only contributes a little bit. That is a huge difference. Women have a larger percentage of fat, necessary for procreation. A woman's percentage of fat has one single purpose: to facilitate lactation. So the hormonal system of women is very different from men's. Secondly, muscle mass is very different in men and women. Men have more muscles than women. This dates back to prehistoric times when men went out hunting. Finally, women's and men's needs differ. Women tend to have a sweet tooth, whereas men prefer salty flavours. Women need more variety, whereas men are generally satisfied with one single course. It suffices to make a few small changes in a man's diet and he will lose weight. Women are more complex. I put forward this theory when I wrote my book Maigrir en gardant la santé... pour les hommes [Losing Weight and Staying Healthy... for Men]. However, it is much more difficult to get a man to exercise than a woman. As far as nutrition is concerned, the main differences occur on the mineral level. Women need more iron, magnesium and calcium. But because men have more muscles, they need more protein.

A distinction is always made between pleasure and nutrition but it is possible to combine both.

I created www.nutrissime.com because I wanted to help people who want to lose weight get rid of their feelings of guilt. Yes, you are allowed to eat a three-course menu without feeling guilty. For all the others (people without any weight to lose), the website is a source of information. They can use it as they like. I do not want to impose any rules, I just want to explain what is within the boundaries of a balanced and nutritious diet.

The recipes on the website are sent in by aficionados, bloggers and chefs alike. So Nutrissime is a real melting-pot. Recipes sent in to Nutrissime are automatically checked and then given a nutritional analysis. They are analysed according to seven food groups. We do not use complicated concepts, such as lipids, carbohydrates etc. We prefer to talk in terms of food groups that you need to consume a certain amount of during the day, for example proteins – fish, meat and eggs – fruit and vegetables, dairy products etc. For each menu, you can check if you have consumed enough of one food group or another and, if necessary, adjust quantities during the next meal. We do not count grams, we prefer to give a general impression of how to create a balanced meal.

Explanatory note on the nutritional information provided with the menus:
The nutritional information provided for the following menus has been calculated on the basis of one person in terms of energy (kcal) and total weight (grams). The information has been calculated with reference to the Guideline Daily Amounts (GDA) and represents the optimum values for an adult having an average daily intake of 2,000 kcal, whereby a main meal (lunch or dinner) consists of 800 to 1,000 kcal. The values mentioned for the following menus conform to European guidelines. The calculations were made by Nutrissime.com.

03 Recipes

Menu 1

This menu contains 985 kcal for a portion of 880 grams.
Your other main meal will also have to contain a portion of protein to create a good balance for the day. This menu contains a good source of fibre, providing more than 68% or 17g of daily requirements. The amount of carbohydrates is satisfactory, providing almost 33% of daily requirements. As this menu contains little added sugar, you are allowed a few sweets during the day.

Green asparagus vichyssoise with black olive purée

Fit the work bowl with the adjustable slicing disc. Peel and halve the potato lengthways. Chop off the root end and green leaves off the leeks. Snap off the woody ends of the asparagus. Slice all the vegetables on the thickest setting on speed 1. Melt the butter in a large saucepan and soften the vegetables on a medium heat. Add the vegetable stock, season and cover the pan. Cook until the vegetables are tender.

Meanwhile, fit the work bowl with the multipurpose blade. When the vegetables are done, purée the contents of the saucepan with the single cream and basil on speed 2. Leave the soup to cool, then refrigerate.

Make the black olive purée. Fit the food processor with the mini-bowl and mini-blade. Stone the olives, then add to the mini-bowl with the peeled and crushed garlic clove, finely chopped thyme and olive oil. Season with salt and pepper. Process on speed 1 until you obtain a smooth purée.

Ladle the asparagus vichyssoise into 4 soup bowls and add a swirl of black olive purée. Garnish with thyme leaves.

Serves 4:
1 medium potato
2 leeks
1 bunch of green asparagus
15 g butter
600 ml vegetable stock
50 ml single cream
1 bunch of basil
fresh thyme leaves, to garnish
salt and freshly ground black pepper

Black olive purée:
115 g Kalamata or Niçoise olives
1 garlic clove
1 sprig of thyme
4 tbsp olive oil

Scan the right page for 'how to make this'-instructions

034 | RECIPES

MENU 1

Serves 4:
320 g lamb fillet
2 lemons
2 onions
2 tsp cumin seeds
50 g butter
a good pinch of pimentón (Spanish smoked paprika)
4 Little Gem lettuces
salt and freshly ground black pepper

White bean hummus:
1 red chilli
a small handful of flat-leaf parsley
2 tbsp extra virgin olive oil
400 g tinned cannellini or haricot beans
4 tbsp white tahini, made from untoasted sesame seeds

LEMON-MARINATED LAMB KEBABS WITH WHITE BEAN HUMMUS

Cut the lamb into 3 cm cubes and place these in a bowl. Fit the food processor with the citrus press. Remove the zest from 1 lemon with a vegetable peeler, then squeeze the juice from both lemons on speed 1. Pour the lemon juice over the lamb. Fit the food processor with the mini-bowl and mini-blade. Process the lemon zest and onions on speed 1, then add to the lamb with the cumin seeds. Season with pepper and mix well. Cover and refrigerate for 1 hour.

Meanwhile, clean the mini-bowl and mini-blade. Deseed the red chilli and process with the parsley and olive oil on speed 1 until finely chopped. Drain and rinse the beans under cold running water. Add to the mini-bowl with the tahini. Process on speed 1 until you obtain a smooth purée. Season to taste with salt. Spoon into a bowl and set aside.

Just before cooking, melt the butter and stir in the paprika. Season. Remove the lamb from the marinade and thread on to 4 skewers. Brush with the paprika butter, season with salt and grill until cooked to your liking. Serve at once with the white bean hummus and Little Gem lettuces.

MENU 1

Serves 4:
50 g sugar
1 tbsp Acacia honey
a pinch of saffron threads
½ vanilla pod
225 ml water
2 Comice pears
juice of ½ lemon
300 g vanilla yoghurt

Polenta crumble:
25 g flour
25 g cold butter
25 g polenta
15 g sugar

SAFFRON PEAR PURÉE WITH VANILLA YOGHURT AND POLENTA CRUMBLE

First make the polenta crumble. Preheat the oven to 180°C. Fit the food processor with the mini-bowl and mini-blade. Add the flour and butter to the mini-bowl and process on speed 1 until the mixture resembles breadcrumbs. Add the polenta and sugar, then process again. Spread the crumble out on a baking sheet lined with greaseproof paper and bake for 15 minutes until light golden and crispy.

For the pear purée, place the sugar, honey, saffron, split vanilla pod and water in a saucepan. Bring to the boil and simmer until the sugar has dissolved. Peel, quarter and core the pears. Add to the syrup and simmer until tender. Meanwhile, clean the mini-bowl and mini-blade. When the pears are done, remove them from the syrup with a slotted spoon and purée with the lemon juice in the mini-bowl on speed 2. Layer the pear purée and vanilla yoghurt in 4 serving glasses. Sprinkle with the polenta crumble.

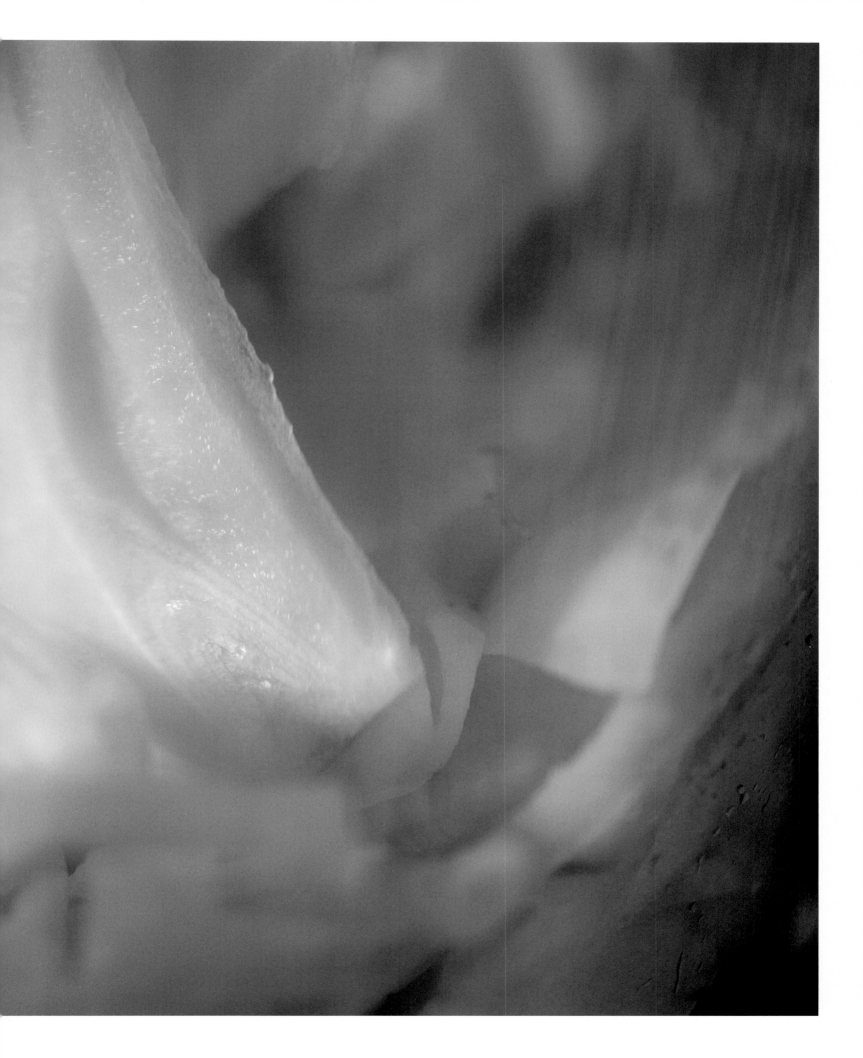

Peel 600 g onions. Slice the onions with the adjustable slicing disc on the medium setting in the work bowl on speed 2. Melt 120 g butter in a large saucepan.

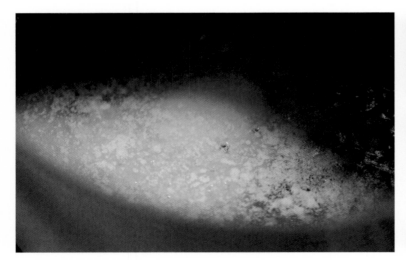 

Add the onions with 6 sprigs of thyme and 1 tbsp honey. Cook on a high heat until the onions start to caramelise. Deglaze the onions with 450 ml dry cider.

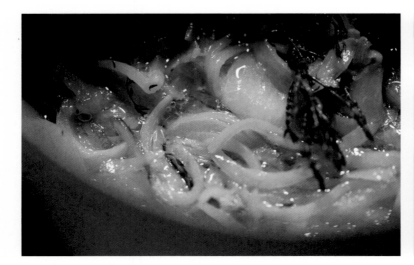 

Add 400 ml chicken stock and simmer until the onions are tender. Purée the onions, without the thyme, with the multifunctional blade in the work bowl on speed 2 until smooth.

 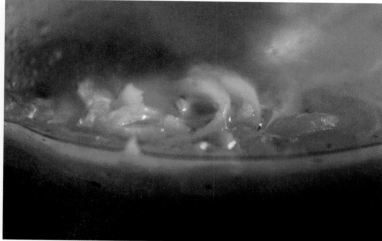

Add 200 ml double cream, purée again and season to taste. Slice 300 g cod fillet into 4 portions.

 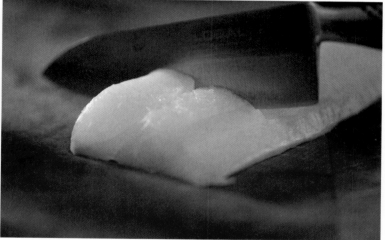

Pan-fry the cod in 2 tbsp olive oil for 2 to 3 minutes on each side. Arrange the cod in 4 soup bowls and pour the onion soup around it.

03 Recipes

Menu 2

This menu contains 1,000 kcal for a portion of 990 grams.
The dishes in this menu are a good source of protein, providing more than 55% of daily requirements, and of omega 3 which is present in the fish. This menu also provides vitamins C and B12, as well as 15 g of fibre.

Serves 4:
250 g onions
2 garlic cloves
2 red chillies
6 lemongrass stalks
25 g coriander
2 tbsp vegetable oil
2 kaffir lime leaves
250 g celeriac
250 g carrots
250 g parsnips
250 g waxy potatoes
750 ml chicken or vegetable stock
250 ml coconut milk
50 ml fish sauce
juice of 1 lime

Root vegetable broth with lemongrass

Fit the food processor with the mini-bowl and mini-blade. Finely chop the onions, garlic, chillies, 2 lemongrass stalks and all the coriander stalks on speed 1. Heat the vegetable oil in a large saucepan and soften the onion mixture for 5 minutes. Bruise the remaining lemongrass stalks and add to the pan with the lime leaves.

Fit the food processor with the dicing kit. Peel and dice the vegetables on speed 1. Add the diced vegetables to the pan and let them soften for 5 minutes. Pour in the stock and coconut milk, bring to the boil and simmer until the vegetables are tender.

Finely chop the coriander leaves. Season the broth with the fish sauce and lime juice, then stir in the coriander. Ladle into 4 soup bowls and serve.

MENU 2

Serves 4:
6 large heads of chicory
1 banana shallot
5 cm ginger
25 g butter
3 tbsp honey
300 ml blood orange juice
100 ml fish stock
1 tbsp olive oil
4 x 125 g sea bass fillets
finely grated orange zest, to garnish
salt and freshly ground black pepper

SEA BASS WITH CHICORY, BLOOD ORANGE AND GINGER COMPOTE

Fit the food processor with the adjustable slicing disc. Remove the outer leaves of the chicory and cut off the root ends, then quarter the chicory heads. Peel the shallot. Slice the chicory and shallot on the thickest setting on speed 1. Peel and finely chop the ginger.

Melt the butter in a large saucepan on a medium heat. Soften the chicory, shallot and ginger for 5 minutes. Stir in the honey, orange juice and fish stock, then turn down the heat. Simmer until the chicory is tender and the liquid has reduced. Season to taste.

Heat the olive oil in a frying pan and fry the sea bass fillets. Season to taste and serve with the chicory compote. Garnish with grated orange zest.

MENU 2

Serves 4:
50 g blanched almonds
25 g blanched hazelnuts
25 g unsalted, shelled pistachio nuts
2 tbsp sugar
½ tsp ground cardamom
4 ripe bananas
4 large sheets of filo pastry
25 g melted butter
4 tbsp fat-free Greek yoghurt, to serve

Green tea syrup:
50 g sugar
100 ml water
¼ tsp matcha (Japanese powdered green tea)
lime juice, to taste

BANANA ROLLS WITH MIXED NUTS AND GREEN TEA SYRUP

Preheat the oven to 180°C. Fit the food processor with the mini-bowl and mini-blade. Process the nuts, sugar and cardamom on speed 1 until finely ground. Peel the bananas, then divide them into two.

Brush each sheet of filo pastry with melted butter, slice in half widthways and then fold each piece of pastry in half vertically. Coat each piece of banana in chopped nuts and place at the end of the pastry rectangles. Roll up, brush with melted butter and sprinkle with more nuts. Place on baking sheets lined with greaseproof paper and bake for 15 minutes until golden brown and crispy.

Meanwhile, stir together the sugar, water and matcha in a small saucepan. Simmer until thickened, then add lime juice to taste. Remove the banana rolls from the oven and serve drizzled with syrup. Place a spoonful of Greek yoghurt on the side. Serve with the remaining nuts.

Halve 6-7 oranges and 1 lemon. Squeeze the oranges with the citrus press in the work bowl on speed 1 and measure 600 ml juice. Squeeze the lemon into the orange juice.

Make a syrup with 150 g sugar and 150 ml water. Measure 300 ml sugar syrup and stir into the citrus juice. Churn in an ice cream machine, then freeze until firm.

Slice off the peel and white pith of 4 oranges and 2 pink grapefruit. Cut between the membranes to remove the segments. Do this over a small saucepan to catch the juices.

Place the segments in a bowl and squeeze the membranes to release the juices. Bring to the boil and reduce until syrupy. Remove from the heat and stir in 3 tbsp Grand Marnier.

Pour over the citrus segments and mix gently. Serve with a scoop of orange sorbet. Finish with fresh mint.

Menu 3

This menu contains 960 kcal for a portion of 750 grams.
The dishes in this vegetarian menu are rich in monounsaturated fats which play an important role in protecting against cardiovascular disease. This menu also contains a good amount of vitamin C and fibre - more than 60% or 16g of daily fibre requirements.

Serves 4:
400 g cooked beetroot
125 g fresh goat's cheese
1 tbsp crème fraîche
2 tbsp blanched hazelnuts
2 handfuls of watercress

Marinade:
4 tbsp extra virgin olive oil
1 tbsp red wine vinegar
1 tsp honey
1 garlic clove, crushed
1 tbsp finely chopped thyme
1 tbsp finely chopped marjoram
salt and freshly ground black pepper

BEETROOT TARTARE WITH GOAT'S CHEESE CREAM, HAZELNUTS AND WATERCRESS

Fit the food processor with the dicing kit. Dice the beetroot on speed 1. Whisk together all the ingredients for the marinade in a bowl. Add the beetroot, toss to combine and marinate at room temperature for 1 hour.

Mix the goat's cheese and crème fraîche in the mini-bowl on speed 1 until smooth. Season to taste. Toast the hazelnuts in a dry pan, then roughly chop them. Just before serving, arrange the beetroot tartare into 4 bowls. Spoon the goat's cheese cream alongside and finish with the toasted hazelnuts and watercress.

MENU 3

Serves 4:
175 g Puy lentils
600 ml vegetable stock
1 red onion
2 garlic cloves
1 red chilli
1 large sprig of rosemary
1 tsp dried oregano
400 g aubergines
400 g courgettes
400 g vine tomatoes
2 tbsp olive oil
50 g sourdough bread
1 bunch of basil
salt and freshly ground black pepper

Parsley oil:
25 g flat-leaf parsley
3 tbsp olive oil
1 tbsp lemon juice

MEDITERRANEAN VEGETABLE GRATIN WITH PUY LENTILS AND PARSLEY OIL

Simmer the Puy lentils in the vegetable stock until just tender, drain and season to taste. Fit the food processor with the mini-bowl and mini-blade. Finely chop the onion, garlic, chilli, rosemary and oregano on speed 1. Stir into the lentils and set aside.

Preheat the oven to 200°C. Fit the food processor with the adjustable slicing disc. Slice the aubergines, courgettes and tomatoes on the thickest setting on speed 1. Preheat a griddle or frying pan and brush the aubergine slices with extra virgin olive oil. Cook the aubergines until tender, then season to taste. Repeat with the courgettes. Spoon the lentils into one large ovenproof dish or 4 individual dishes, if you prefer. Layer the cooked aubergines and courgettes and raw tomatoes on top.

Process the sourdough bread and basil in the mini-bowl on speed 2. Sprinkle all over the vegetables and bake for 15 to 20 minutes. Meanwhile, make the parsley oil by mixing all the ingredients in the mini-bowl on speed 2. Season with salt, then serve with the vegetable gratin.

MENU 3

Serves 4:
4 x 7.5 cm shortcrust pastry circles
2 small bananas
juice of ½ lime
2 tsp sugar
grated orange zest, to garnish

Rhubarb purée:
200 g pink rhubarb
2 cm ginger
25 g sugar

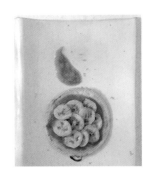

CARAMELISED BANANA TARTLETS WITH RHUBARB PURÉE

First prepare the rhubarb purée. Peel and roughly chop the rhubarb and ginger. Place in a saucepan with the sugar. Bring to the boil, then simmer until the rhubarb is tender. Fit the food processor with mini-bowl and mini-blade. Purée the rhubarb and ginger on speed 1 until smooth. Leave to cool.

Preheat the oven to 190°C. Place the pastry circles on a baking sheet lined with greaseproof paper. Prick the pastry all over with a fork and bake for 5 minutes until lightly coloured. Spread the rhubarb purée on to the pastry but leave the edges free.

Fit the food processor with the adjustable slicing disc. Peel the bananas and slice them on the thickest setting on speed 1. Toss with the lime juice and arrange on the rhubarb purée. Sprinkle with the sugar and bake for 10 minutes until the bananas are cooked. Garnish with grated orange zest and serve.

Dissolve 7 g dried yeast in 100 ml lukewarm water. Sift 300 g '00' flour into the work bowl with the dough blade. Add a little salt and 90 g diced butter. Pour in 1 beaten egg and the yeast mixture.

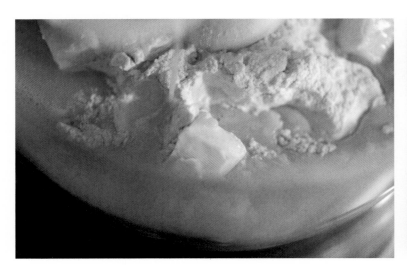

Mix on speed 1 until the dough forms a ball. Place in a bowl, cover and leave to rise until doubled in volume. Peel and slice 1 kg red onions with the adjustable slicing disc on the medium setting on speed 2. Heat 4 tbsp olive oil in a large pan and soften the onions.

Add 4 sliced garlic cloves, 6 sprigs of thyme, 2 tbsp balsamic vinegar and 2 tbsp honey. Season, cover the pan and cook on a low heat for 20 minutes until the onions are tender. Knock back the dough, knead briefly and roll out.

Place on an oiled baking sheet, spread with the onion mixture and arrange 100 g anchovy fillets on top in a criss-cross pattern. Bake for 20 minutes in a preheated oven at 200°C.

Slice 4-5 plum tomatoes with the adjustable slicing disc on the thickest setting on speed 1. Arrange on the pissaladière and bake for another 20 minutes. Serve sprinkled with thyme.

03 RECIPES

MENU 4

This menu contains 1,000 kcal for a portion of 760 grams.
Rich in protein, this menu provides almost 70% of daily requirements. Be sure to reduce your portion of protein at the next meal to balance your intake for the day. This menu also provides a good amount of fruits and vegetables rich in vitamin C.

Serves 4:
3 blood oranges
2 small fennel bulbs
½ red onion
50 g pitted Kalamata olives
½ bunch of dill
1 tbsp white wine vinegar
50 ml extra virgin olive oil
100 g manouri (or feta) cheese
salt and freshly ground black pepper

FENNEL, BLOOD ORANGE AND RED ONION SALAD WITH MANOURI CHEESE

Slice off the peel and white pith of 2 oranges, then cut between the membranes to remove the segments; do this over a small saucepan to catch the juice. When all the segments have been removed, set them aside and squeeze the empty membranes to release the juice. Grate the zest from the remaining orange and set aside, then squeeze the juice and add to the saucepan. Bring to the boil and reduce until syrupy. Leave to cool.

Fit the food processor with the adjustable slicing disc. Remove the green stalks from the fennel and peel the red onion. Slice the fennel and onion on the thinnest setting on speed 1. Place in a large bowl and mix with the blood orange segments. Fit the food processor with the mini-bowl and mini-blade. Roughly chop the olives and dill on speed 1. Add to the bowl.

Stir together the reduced blood orange juice, vinegar and olive oil. Add the reserved orange zest and season to taste. Add to the salad and toss gently to combine. Leave for 30 minutes, so the flavours have time to develop. Just before serving, spoon into 4 bowls and crumble the manouri cheese on top.

MENU 4

Serves 4:
1 small shallot
25 g capers
grated zest of ½ lemon
a small handful of flat-leaf parsley
350 g turkey mince
1 tbsp olive oil
4 sesame-topped burger buns
a handful of rocket leaves
salt and freshly ground black pepper

Tonnato cream:
3 anchovy fillets in olive oil
50 g tinned tuna in olive oil
1 tbsp capers
2 tbsp lemon juice
2 tbsp chopped flat-leaf parsley
200 g crème fraîche

TURKEY BURGERS WITH TONNATO CREAM

Fit the food processor with the mini-bowl and mini-blade. Process the shallot, capers, lemon zest and parsley on speed 1. Mix into the turkey mince and season with salt and pepper. Shape into 4 burgers about 1 cm thick.

Drain the anchovy fillets and tuna. Place in the mini-bowl with the capers, lemon juice and parsley. Process on speed 2. Add the crème fraîche and process on pulse until just combined. Season to taste and chill.

Cook the turkey burgers in the olive oil on a griddle or in a frying pan. Serve on toasted burger buns with the tonnato cream and rocket leaves.

MENU 4

Serves 4:
375 ml milk
375 ml water
3 egg whites
75 g vanilla sugar (made with fresh vanilla)
a pinch of salt
25 g unsalted, shelled pistachio nuts
finely diced strawberry, to garnish

Strawberry-gin coulis:
250 g strawberries
75 g Acacia honey
2 tbsp Hendrick's (or other) gin

FLOATING ISLANDS WITH STRAWBERRY-GIN COULIS

First make the strawberry-gin coulis. Fit the food processor with the mini-bowl and mini-blade. Wash and hull the strawberries, then place them in the mini-bowl. Add the honey and gin. Process on speed 2 until you obtain a smooth purée. Push through a non-metallic sieve and set aside.

Pour the milk and water in a wide, shallow saucepan and bring to a gentle simmer. Make sure the work bowl is absolutely free of grease and fit it with the egg whip. Add the egg whites and whisk on speed 2 until they form soft peaks. Keep the motor running and slowly add the vanilla sugar and salt until you obtain a glossy meringue.

Using two small tablespoons, shape the meringue into quenelles and gently drop these into the hot milk. Poach the meringues for 1 minute on each side; cook four meringues at a time. Scoop the cooked meringues out of the liquid with a slotted spoon and drain on kitchen paper. Pour the strawberry coulis into each plate and place 2 to 3 meringues on top. Sprinkle with chopped pistachio nuts and garnish with diced strawberry. Serve at once.

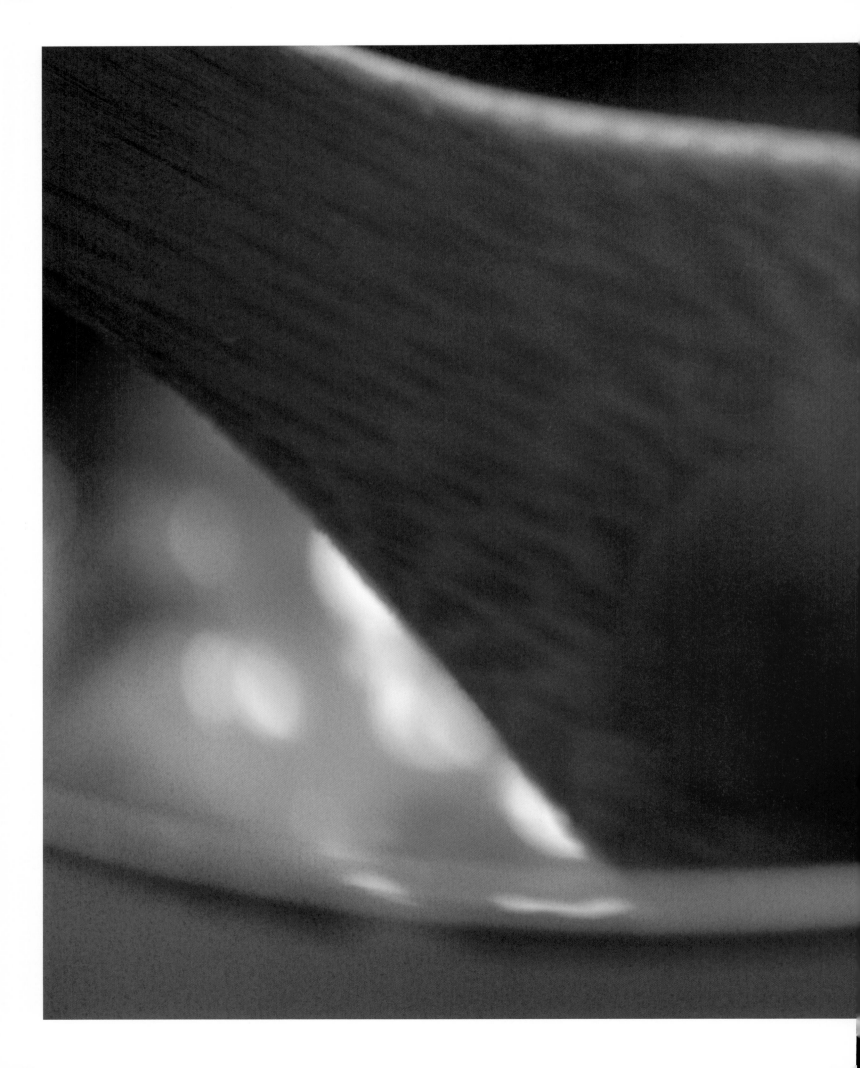

Peel 500 g carrots, top and tail 1 bunch of turnips. Slice the carrots with the adjustable slicing disc on the medium setting in the work bowl on speed 1. Boil the carrots until tender to the bite, drain and set aside in a bowl.

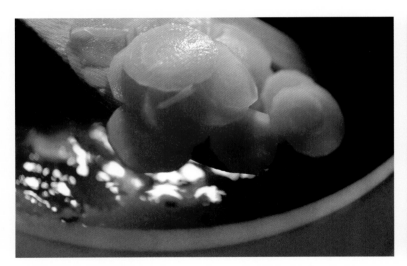

Mix together 6 tbsp olive oil and 2 tbsp cider vinegar. Season. Toss the carrots with the vinaigrette while warm. Dice the turnips with the dicing kit on speed 1.

Blanch the turnips in salted water for 1 minute, then drain. Stir the turnips into the carrot salad.

Season with 1 tbsp honey. Finely chop ½ bunch of dill, stir into 125 g fromage frais and add 1 tbsp creamed horseradish.

Gently fold the vegetables into a couple of handfuls of rocket. Serve the root vegetable salad with the herby fromage frais.

Start eating vegetables as early in life as possible.

I am a medical doctor and journalist. I graduated as a GP in 1987 but found the job to be quite lonely, so I went to Africa to practice 'bush medicine'. But that was not what I was looking for either, so I came back in search of new challenges. I landed a job in the media purely by coincidence, with a specialist publication, and that is when I found my feet. That was twenty years ago. I started out by writing for the trade press and then branched out for a wider audience, which is what I prefer. I began working for Roularta Media Group six years ago, which is when I started up Bodytalk, a magazine about healthy eating, psychology, sport and good health in general.

Fruit and vegetables are very healthy but we eat too little of them. I always say that you should divide your plate into two: fill half of it with vegetables, a quarter with fish, meat or – if you are a vegetarian – a meat substitute, and another quarter with rice, pasta or potatoes. If you do that, you are eating even more vegetables than the food pyramid prescribes. But I think that in future we will have to start thinking more about sustainability. We eat too much meat and fish, too few fruit and vegetables. It is a good rule, I try to apply it myself. We should aim to eat two pieces of fruit and three portions of vegetables a day. A portion of fruit is a handful of grapes or cherries, a portion of vegetables is a heaped tablespoon.

Vegetables contain a lot of fibre, vitamins and minerals. Fibre is important for the functioning of the intestines. If you only eat well-done meat, potatoes, white rice and bread, you are guaranteed to get intestinal troubles such as constipation and cramps. So you must eat fibre, this will also help to ease the transit of other nutrients.
We also need vitamins. Scurvy is a disease which used to rage on ships where fresh fruit and vegetables were lacking. This type of disease is as good as extinct in the Western world. Real vitamin shortages are rare and only occur in people with very monotonous diets:

Dr Marleen Finoulst graduated as a GP in 1987. After a short stint in Africa she landed a job in the media and now heads Bodytalk, a magazine aimed at a wide audience about health, psychology and eating well.

students who are in the middle of exams, the chronically ill... How can you tell if someone is suffering from a vitamin shortage? Brittle nails, lacklustre hair, mouth ulcers, etc.

A connection has been made in the last ten to twenty years between a shortage of vitamin D and brittle bones. People tend to stay inside more during winter: they get into their car straight from the office and then drive straight home. They do not go outside any more, which means there is less contact with the sun – vitamin D is created by exposure to the sun. People also use stronger day creams with sun protection factors which cancel out the sun's health benefits. You need a little sunlight, in winter too. Skin cancer is a danger in the summer, when there is a lot of exposure to the sun. You cannot say: I'll store up a reserve of vitamin D in the summer, you have to stock up on it every day. Ideally, you should go outside for fifteen to twenty minutes every day.

There has been some epidemiological research into the question of whether fruit and vegetables protect against cancer. If we divide people into groups eating a lot of, few or no fruit and vegetables, it is clear that the first group is better protected against certain types of cancers. Particularly colon and stomach cancer, perhaps because of the fibre content of fruit and vegetables. But no connection has been discovered with breast or lung cancer. To enjoy the beneficial effects against cancer in general, it is important to start eating fruit and vegetables as early on in life as possible. Indirectly, fruit and vegetables protect against cardiovascular disease, as they contain few calories. Their fibre content also means that they leave you feeling full. In that sense, fruit and vegetables are good for the cardiovascular system because they stop you from eating too many fats.

Broccoli and blueberries are said to be 'superfoods' but this is disputed. Vegetables are important, in general. You should not eat too monotonously, variety is very important. Yes, broccoli is healthy but so is lettuce. So, no, there are no real 'super foods'. But if we single out specific nutrients, some ingredients do score very high. Strawberries, kiwi fruit and blueberries, for example, contain extremely high levels of vitamin C, more than oranges even. If you are healthy, you will radiate this. By eating enough fruit and vegetables, all your organs will benefit – the skin is an organ, as well – including your hair and nails. Are there any food products we can single out as being particularly beneficial? No, once more: it is important to eat enough fruit and vegetables.

The quality of frozen vegetables, even tinned vegetables, is very good these days. There is so much competition that the difference between fresh and frozen is minimal, as far as taste and vitamin content are concerned. The very best remains: organic vegetables, freshly picked from your garden and brought straight to your plate. But they are not available to everyone. In second place come fresh vegetables from the supermarket. Or maybe not... because how fresh will they be if you leave them hanging around your fridge for days on end? Whereas frozen vegetables are frozen straight after being harvested. In that case you are better off buying fresh vegetables for the first couple of days and frozen veg for later on in the week.

New food theories are launched every single day, for example the paleo diet (eating like prehistoric man). They are real fads and at Bodytalk we receive dozens of questions about them. But fads come and go. Raw is certainly not the best way to eat vegetables, you would run into any number of intestinal problems if you were to eat everything raw. The human body is not designed for it. The alkaline diet is plain wrong. It is true that there are acidic and alkaline food products but our blood has a constant ph-value. If the ph-value of your blood were to become very acidic or very alkaline, that would mean that you were very ill indeed! When you eat acidic ingredients, the balance of your blood is immediately

We should aim to eat two pieces of fruit and three portions of vegetables a day.

regulated. So the alkaline diet is complete nonsense. You could compare it to our body temperature: that remains at a constant 37°C, as well.

That is the danger: people get tired of all these diets. Research has been done into this by the University of Ghent. When people receive too much contradictory information about food, they also tend to dispense with their good eating habits.

To prevent obesity we have to teach our children to eat more fruit and vegetables. As far as fruit is concerned, obligatory fruit days at primary schools are a great success. This is an initiative whereby once a week children have to bring a piece of fruit to school instead of biscuits or crisps. It is a good way to make children eat more fruit. Some schools buy fruit and then distribute it or sell it on, so you can buy an apple for very little money. Something which also helps are snack boxes in the shape of a banana, as bananas bruise very easily when carried around in satchels and children love them.
It is a great idea to arrange vegetables on the plate in the shape of a face, with cherry tomatoes for eyes etc. Children's cookbooks are interesting because they show you how to cook in a playful way with healthy ingredients. Also, mix vegetables into mashed potatoes. My children hate Brussels sprouts but mixed with mashed potatoes they absolutely love them. It is a good way to get children to experience new flavours. But do not try everything at once. People sometimes think that their baby has to taste as many different flavours as possible. Take things slowly. If you try too much at once, children are at risk of developing aversions.

RECIPE 1

Serves 4-6:
2 medium aubergines
2 tbsp olive oil
400 g tinned chickpeas
2 green celery stalks
2 mint sprigs
2 tbsp golden raisins
1 tbsp white balsamic vinegar
4 tbsp ricotta cheese
2-3 tsp fresh pesto
4-6 ciabatta slices
salt and freshly ground black pepper

Tomato salsa:
375 g vine tomatoes
1 garlic clove
1 tbsp red wine vinegar
2 tbsp lemon-flavoured olive oil

AUBERGINE AND CHICKPEA CAPONATA WITH HERB RICOTTA CROSTINI

Fit the food processor with the dicing kit. Dice the aubergines on speed 1, then gently fry the diced aubergines in the olive oil until tender. Drain the chickpeas. Finely chop the celery and mint. Stir together the cooked aubergines, chickpeas, celery, mint and raisins in a large bowl. Season with the balsamic vinegar, salt and pepper.

Fit the food processor with the mini-bowl and mini-blade. Finely chop the tomatoes with the garlic, vinegar and olive oil speed 1. Season to taste. Stir into the caponata and leave at room temperature for the flavours to develop.

Stir together the ricotta and pesto. Toast the ciabatta slices and spread with the herb ricotta. Arrange the caponata on 4 to 6 plates and serve the crostini on the side.

This Italian aubergine and chickpea salad will provide useful minerals (potassium and folic acid), while the tomatoes contain plenty of vitamin C.

RECIPE 2

Serves 4:
450 g whites of leeks
300 g green asparagus
100 g diced smoky bacon
a few chives, to garnish

Truffle gribiche:
3 organic eggs, at room temperature
1 tsp capers
1 tsp wholegrain mustard
1 sprig of tarragon
½ bunch of dill
1 tbsp tarragon vinegar
2 tbsp olive oil
1 tbsp truffle oil
salt and freshly ground black pepper

STEAMED LEEKS AND ASPARAGUS WITH TRUFFLE GRIBICHE

First make the truffle gribiche. Bring a small saucepan of water to the boil, then gently lower the eggs into it. Boil the eggs for 10 minutes. Meanwhile, fit the food processor with the mini-bowl and mini-blade. Finely chop the capers, mustard, tarragon, dill, vinegar, olive and truffle oils on speed 2. Refresh the eggs under cold running water; this will prevent a dark circle appearing around the yolks. Peel the eggs, then slice them into quarters and add them to the mini-bowl. Process on speed 1 until the eggs are finely chopped. Season to taste.

Remove the outer leaves of the leeks. Snap off the woody ends of the asparagus. Fit the food processor with the adjustable slicing disc. Slice the leeks and asparagus on the thickest setting on speed 1. Steam the leeks and asparagus until tender to the bite. Keep warm.

Fry the bacon in a dry pan until golden brown. Arrange the steamed vegetables and bacon on 4 plates and spoon the truffle gribiche alongside. Garnish with chopped chives.

Asparagus provides heaps of nutrients, such as vitamins A, B1, B2 and C, while leeks contain plenty of iron. Combined with the protein in the eggs, this dish is a real power starter.

RECIPE 3

Serves 4:
15 g dried hijiki (or arame) seaweed
1 cucumber
125 g button mushrooms
200 g daikon radish
400 g squid

Wasabi dressing:
50 ml lime juice
2 tbsp mirin (Japanese sweet rice wine)
1.5 tsp light soy sauce
1 tsp matcha (Japanese powdered green tea)
1 tsp wasabi paste

JAPANESE SALAD WITH WASABI DRESSING AND GRILLED SQUID

Soak the seaweed in cold water for 5 minutes, drain and put in a saucepan with just enough water to cover. Simmer for 20 minutes, drain once more and leave to cool. Whisk together all the ingredients for the dressing.

Fit the food processor with the adjustable slicing disc. Peel the daikon and halve the cucumber lengthways. Wipe the mushrooms clean and trim the stalks. Slice the daikon, cucumber and mushrooms on the medium setting on speed 1. Toss the vegetables and seaweed with the wasabi dressing. Leave to marinate while you prepare the squid.

Clean the squid by removing the quills and tentacles, then slit the bodies open on one side. Open them and lay them flat, trimming the edges to form triangles. Rinse the squid bodies under cold running water and pat dry. Score the bodies with a grid pattern and lightly brush with vegetable oil. Heat a frying pan until very hot, then cook the squid for 30 seconds. Turn over and grill for 10 more seconds.

Just before serving, drain the salad and spoon on to 4 plates. Arrange the squid on top and finish with a drizzle of wasabi dressing.

This Japanese-style salad is a great source of vitamins, namely B1 and B2 in the shape of the squid, and vitamin C with the cucumber and daikon radish.

RECIPE 4

Serves 4-6:
1 floury potato
1 parsnip
2 carrots
75 g Savoy cabbage
a small handful of flat-leaf parsley
1 large sprig of rosemary
3 tbsp melted butter
1 sheet of ready-rolled puff pastry
1 egg
2 tsp poppy seeds
salt and freshly ground black pepper

Garlic cream:
2 green garlic bulbs
100 ml whole milk

WINTER VEGETABLE STRUDEL WITH GREEN GARLIC CREAM

Preheat the oven to 210°C. Fit the food processor with the adjustable slicing disc. Peel and slice the vegetables on the medium setting on speed 1. Shred the cabbage. Finely chop the flat-leaf parsley and rosemary. Blanch the sliced vegetables and cabbage in boiling salted water for 5 to 10 minutes, or until tender. Drain, then mix in a large bowl with the melted butter and chopped herbs. Season to taste.

Roll out the pastry and arrange the vegetables in the middle, leaving the edges free. Fold the pastry over the vegetables. Lightly beat the egg and use to glaze the pastry. Sprinkle with the poppy seeds and place on a baking sheet lined with baking paper. Bake for 20 to 25 minutes until golden brown and crispy.

Meanwhile, make the garlic cream. Remove the outer layer of skin from the garlic and roughly chop the bulb. Place in a saucepan and add the milk with a pinch of salt. Bring to the boil and simmer gently until the garlic is tender. Tip the contents of the saucepan into the mini-bowl and purée on speed 2 until smooth. Push through a fine sieve, season to taste and keep warm.

Remove the vegetable strudel from the oven and leave for 10 minutes before carving into 4 to 6 portions. Serve with the garlic cream.

This dish is not for the faint-hearted, as it contains lots of garlic. But it is good for you too, as garlic is thought to protect against coronary heart disease.

Wash 600 g cherry tomatoes. Slice the tomatoes with the adjustable slicing disc on the thickest setting in the prep bowl on speed 1. Rinse and top and tail 1 bunch of radishes, then slice on the medium setting on speed 1.

Add 2 tbsp olive oil, 1 tsp red wine vinegar and ½ tsp salt. Set aside. Place 1 garlic clove, 1 tsp salt, 2 anchovy fillets, 1 tsp mustard, 1 tbsp capers, 1 bunch of basil, ½ bunch of mint, ½ bunch of flat-leaf parsley in the mini-bowl.

Mix on speed 2 with 4 tbsp olive oil and 2 tbsp lemon juice, then season. Coarsely crush 2 tbsp black peppercorns with a pestle and mortar.

Rub into two 250 g boneless rib-eye steaks. Heat 1 tbsp olive oil and 1 tbsp butter in a frying pan on a high heat. Cook the steak until rare, then season with salt.

Rest the steak for 5 to 10 minutes, then slice into strips. Arrange the tomato and radish salad on 4 plates, top with the tagliata and salsa verde.

RECIPE 5

Serves 4:
800 g broccoli
4 tbsp ricotta
150 ml lobster stock
2 tbsp double cream
25 g cold butter
25 g trout roe
a squeeze of lemon juice
12 large langoustines (Dublin Bay prawns)
court-bouillon, to cook the langoustines
toasted flaked almonds, to garnish
freshly ground black pepper and sea salt

BROCCOLI PURÉE WITH LANGOUSTINES AND TROUT ROE JUS

Fit the food processor with the multipurpose blade. Divide the broccoli into florets and cook these in salted boiling water until tender. Drain and purée the broccoli with the ricotta on speed 2. Keep warm.

Cook the lobster stock and double cream in a small saucepan until reduced by half. Remove from the heat and whisk in the cold butter until slightly thickened, then stir through the trout roe. Season with a squeeze of lemon juice, salt and pepper. Keep warm.

Boil the langoustines in court-bouillon until just cooked. Spoon the broccoli purée on to 4 plates. Place the langoustines on top and drizzle with the sauce. Garnish with flaked almonds.

Broccoli is a vegetable to be reckoned with, containing significant quantities of vitamin C, potassium, iron and folic acid. And so quick to prepare!

RECIPE 6

Serves 4:
2 tbsp softened butter
1 tsp wholegrain mustard
1 garlic clove
1 sprig of sage
zest of ½ lemon
4 x 100 g chicken breast fillets with skin
salt and freshly ground black pepper

Sweet potatoes:
750 g sweet potatoes
1 tbsp vegetable oil
1 tbsp butter
1 onion
50 g pancetta
250 g baby spinach leaves

Honey jus:
3 tbsp honey
100 ml chicken stock
1 bay leaf
1 tbsp butter
juice of ½ lemon

MUSTARD-ROAST CHICKEN WITH SWEET POTATOES, SPINACH AND HONEY JUS

Preheat the oven to 200°C. Fit the food processor with the mini-bowl and mini-blade. Process the butter, mustard, garlic, sage and lemon zest on speed 2 until smooth. Season to taste. Rub the mustard butter underneath the chicken skin. Arrange the chicken breasts in a roasting tin and bake for 20 minutes.

Fit the food processor with the dicing kit. Peel and dice the sweet potatoes on speed 1. Heat the oil and butter in a large pan on a medium heat. Finely chop the onion and pancetta, then cook until softened. Add the sweet potatoes, cover the pan and cook until the potatoes are tender. At the last minute, stir in the spinach leaves and cook until just wilted. Season to taste and keep warm.

Make the honey jus. Place the honey, chicken stock and bay leaf in a saucepan and simmer until reduced by two-thirds. Whisk in the butter and season with the lemon juice, salt and pepper. Keep warm.

Remove the chicken breasts from the oven and place on 4 plates. Arrange the sweet potatoes and spinach alongside, then spoon the honey jus all around. Serve at once.

Sweet potatoes are a great source of vitamin A and in combination with the vitamin C and iron provided by spinach, this dish is not to be underestimated.

RECIPE 7

Serves 4:
2 large carrots
1 courgette
150 g frozen peas
250 g linguine (or spaghetti)
1 tbsp olive oil
4 x 100 g veal escalopes

Lemon-basil sauce:
juice of 2 lemons
75 ml olive oil
75 g Parmesan cheese
1 bunch of basil
salt and freshly ground black pepper

SPRING VEGETABLE, LEMON AND BASIL LINGUINE WITH VEAL ESCALOPE

First make the lemon-basil sauce. Fit the food processor with the mini-bowl and mini-blade. Process all the ingredients on speed 2 until well-mixed. Season to taste and set aside.

Fit the food processor with the reversible shredding disc, fine side up. Peel the carrot and top and tail the courgette. Shred the vegetables on speed 1. Set aside. Let the peas defrost. Cook the pasta al dente in boiling salted water. Drain, then immediately toss with the shredded vegetables, defrosted peas and sauce. The heat of the pasta will partially cook the vegetables.

Heat the olive oil in a frying pan and cook the veal escalopes on a high heat. Season to taste and serve with the spring vegetable linguine.

Lemons are an important source of vitamin C. Combined with the vitamin A provided by crunchy grated carrots and courgettes, this pasta dish is very good for you indeed.

Scan the right page for 'how to make this'-instructions

Recipe 8

Serves 4:
2 rosehip tea bags
400 ml boiling water
100 g sugar
450 g mixed red berries, for example
strawberries, raspberries and redcurrants
seeds from 1 pomegranate, to garnish

Melon and basil sorbet:
1 ripe Charentais or cantaloupe melon
250 ml sugar syrup (made with equal
quantities sugar and water)
½ bunch of basil
2 tbsp lemon juice
1 egg white

Red berry gazpacho with melon and basil sorbet

Place the tea bags in a measuring jug. Add the water and sugar, stirring until the sugar has dissolved. Leave to infuse for 10 minutes. Fit the food processor with the multipurpose blade, then add the washed berries. Pour in the rosehip syrup and purée the fruit on speed 2. Push the purée through a non-metallic sieve into a bowl and refrigerate.

Clean the work bowl and multipurpose blade. Halve the melon and scoop out the seeds, then slice the flesh from the rind. Roughly chop the flesh and purée on speed 2 with the sugar syrup and basil. Pour into a measuring jug and chill.

When the melon purée has been thoroughly chilled, churn in an ice-cream machine for 10 minutes. Lightly beat the egg white and add to the ice-cream machine while the motor is running. Continue churning for another 10 minutes. Pour the berry gazpacho into 4 deep plates and place a scoop of melon sorbet in the middle. Sprinkle with pomegranate seeds and serve.

Whoever said desserts were bad for you? Red berries are positively bursting with vitamin C, so every mouthful of this gazpacho not only tastes good but will have you glowing with health.

RECIPE 9

Serves 4:
½ large, ripe pineapple (see below)
6 tbsp white rum
1 tsp cracked pink peppercorns
desiccated coconut, to garnish

Tropical fruit frozen yoghurt:
1 large, ripe pineapple
1 banana
25 g fresh coconut flesh
100 g light brown sugar
2 tbsp white rum
250 g natural yoghurt
juice from ½ lime

GRILLED PINEAPPLE WITH RUM AND TROPICAL FRUIT FROZEN YOGHURT

First make the frozen yoghurt. Fit the work bowl with the multipurpose blade. Top and tail the pineapple, then place the fruit on a chopping board. Using a large serrated knife, cut off the skin from top to bottom. Slice the pineapple lengthways into quarters and remove the fibrous core. Set aside two quarters and chop the rest into chunks.

Peel and chop the banana. Place the pineapple and banana in the work bowl. Add the remaining ingredients for the frozen yoghurt and mix on speed 2 until smooth. Churn in an ice-cream machine for 15 minutes, then freeze until firm enough to serve.

Clean the work bowl and fit it with the adjustable slicing disc. Slice the remaining two pineapple quarters on the thickest setting on speed 1, then place the slices in a bowl. Add the white rum and pink peppercorns, toss and marinate for 20 minutes.

Just before serving, preheat a griddle pan until very hot. Grill the pineapple slices for 1 to 2 minutes until caramelised. Serve with a scoop of frozen yoghurt. Sprinkle with desiccated coconut and serve at once.

Pineapple and banana are a great combo, as they provide vitamins B and C and their fibre content keeps your body healthy too. What's more, they taste great!

Sift 200 g flour and a little salt into the work bowl with the multifunctional blade. Add 100 g diced cold butter. Process on speed 1 until the mixture resembles breadcrumbs. Add 4 tbsp cold water and mix until the dough forms a ball. Chill for 1 hour.

Peel and grate 600 g carrots with the reversible shredding disc, medium side up, on speed 2. Finely chop 1 onion. Heat 2 tbsp olive oil in a large pan and soften the carrots and onion.

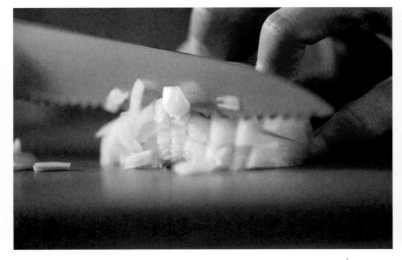 

Add ½ tsp salt and 200 ml chicken stock and cook until the liquid evaporates. Remove from the heat. Beat 3 eggs, add 100 g crumbled goat's cheese and 1 finely chopped bunch of coriander.

Fold into the cooled carrot mixture. Season with pepper. Roll out the pastry and line a 20 cm loose-based tart tin.

Fill with the carrot mixture and bake for 35 minutes in a preheated oven at 200°C. Serve with a watercress salad.

Foodpairing is the ideal tool to open up a world of new possibilities

Bernard Lahousse Scientist by trade and foodie by nature, Bernard Lahousse developed Foodpairing, a new approach to food combining based on the scientific analysis of aromas. It is now used by chefs all over the world.

Chef Peter Coucquyt spent twenty years honing his skills in Michelin-starred restaurants (Hof van Cleve, Kasteel Withof) before joining forces with Bernard Lahousse and taking Foodpairing to a new level.

I am Peter Coucquyt, a graduate from Ter Duinen catering college in Koksijde, Belgium. After completing my apprenticeships, I spent sixteen years at the Michelin-starred restaurant Hof van Cleve in Kruishoutem. I started out front-of-house but after three years I made the transition to the kitchen, helping to develop it into what it is now. After Hof van Cleve I set up Kasteel Withof in Brasschaat, staying on for four years and earning a Michelin star in the process. During my time at Kasteel Withof I started working with Bernard. I met Bernard at a wine symposium where he was one of the guest speakers.

B: That was one of my first talks about foodpairing.

P: A subject which interested me because cooking and science have always been two passions of mine. I was already reading articles and books about them back in the days of Hof van Cleve.

B: I did not train as a chef like Peter, however. I have a scientific background, being a bioscience engineer. However, I have always had a strong passion for gastronomy. I love to eat and cook. I'm a real foodie. I used to cook quite a lot but now I don't have as much time as I used to. I even took part in a major cooking competition once. Foodpairing came about because I started talking to chefs like Kobe Desramaults from In de Wulf and Sang-Hoon Degeimbre from L'Air du Temps and noticed that they were interested in creating new combinations. So I started researching the subject with the aid of the IWT [Agency for Innovation through Science and Technology]. But not just every top chef in Flanders uses it, Heston Blumenthal (The Fat Duck, UK) and Ferran Adrià (El Bullì, Spain) work with it, as well. And foodpairing is also being extended to bartending, a strong new trend at the moment.

INTERVIEW ABOUT FOODPAIRING

*Cooking, whether you like it
or not, is chemistry.
It's all about molecules.*

B: What is foodpairing? It is the analysis of food products in a scientific manner. By means of the aromatic profile obtained we can determine which combinations are possible and, moreover, which combinations are more likely than others. Foodpairing is applied by means of foodpairing 'trees'. The main ingredient is placed in the middle and all the ingredients with which it can be combined are placed around it in clusters: drinks, dairy products, meat etc. Distance is also an important factor: the closer to the main ingredient, the more successful the combination. That is how you can create endless combinations.

B: The scientific analysis of the products is carried out by a university. Explaining how aromas are analysed would be too technical but there are machines that can do this. We then feed the data into our database which compares it to 1,300 other ingredients which have been analysed previously. Foodpairing is a tool which is primarily used by professional chefs because you need a certain knowledge of cooking to be able to combine asparagus and lychees, for example. That said, there some foodies amongst our users. About ten per cent of users of our website www.foodpairing.com are passionate foodies who are clearly interested in the tools used by top chefs to create unusual combinations.
P: The hardest thing about foodpairing is finding the right balance between the ingredients you have chosen. Whether it is a dish or a drink you want to create, the balance must be right. For a foodie this is more difficult because they do not have the same culinary background a professional chef has. But a professional can also experience problems in finding the right balance with foodpairing, you know. That's why it is best not to combine more than five ingredients at once.
B: However, you can make it easier on yourself by working with juices. For example, if you go to the website and type in 'apple-cranberry juice', you'll get a list of ingredients that are a good match: coriander, peppermint, basil, cardamom, rosemary. Juices are easier to work with than complete dishes.

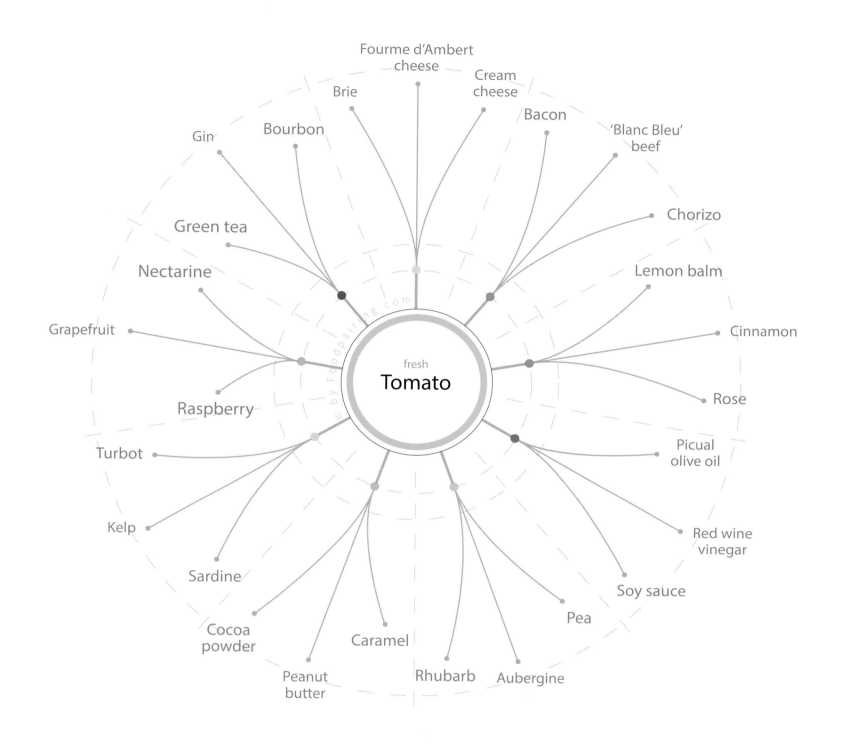

Fourme d'Ambert cheese
Cream cheese
Brie
Bacon
Bourbon
'Blanc Bleu' beef
Gin
Chorizo
Green tea
Lemon balm
Nectarine
Cinnamon
Grapefruit
fresh
Tomato
Rose
Raspberry
Picual olive oil
Turbot
Red wine vinegar
Kelp
Soy sauce
Sardine
Pea
Cocoa powder
Caramel
Peanut butter
Rhubarb
Aubergine

© by Foodpairing.com

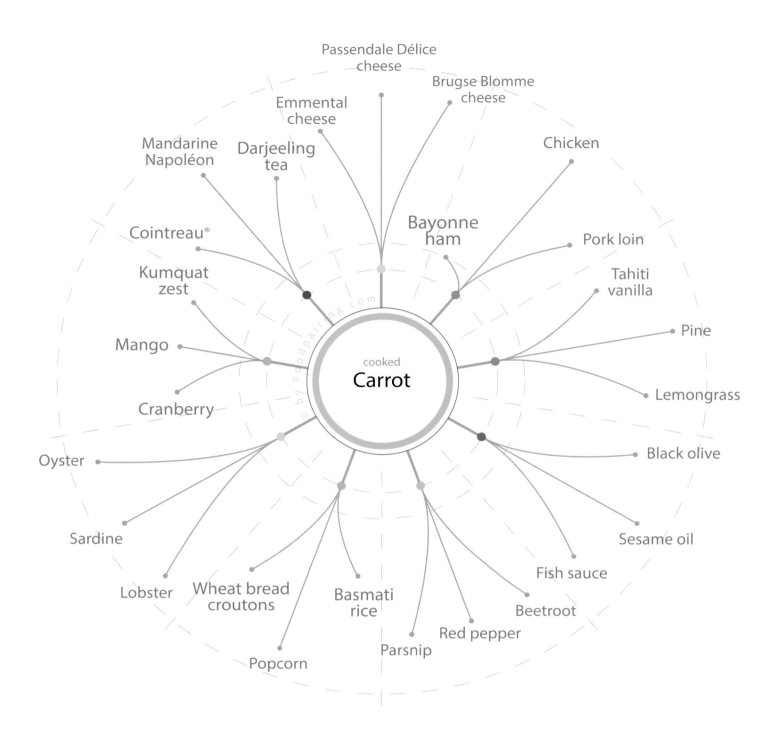

Passendale Délice cheese

Brugse Blomme cheese

Emmental cheese

Chicken

Mandarine Napoléon

Darjeeling tea

Cointreau®

Bayonne ham

Pork loin

Kumquat zest

Tahiti vanilla

cooked
Carrot

Pine

Mango

Lemongrass

Cranberry

Black olive

Oyster

Sesame oil

Sardine

Fish sauce

Lobster

Wheat bread croutons

Basmati rice

Beetroot

Popcorn

Parsnip

Red pepper

B: There is a great deal of difference between different varieties of the same product. An apple is not just an apple, a strawberry is not just a strawberry. Whether you fry or boil an ingredient has an influence on the aroma, as well. Cookery, whether you like it or not, is chemistry. It is all about molecules. If you pan-fry a steak, hundreds of new molecules are created. Some are nutty, which means that you can combine the steak with almonds or cherries. Others are toasty, meaning you can pair the steak with coffee or chocolate.

B: All the recipes on the website are free, as well as one hundred ingredients that you can study by means of their foodpairing trees. To see the thousand or so other ingredients, you must pay a membership fee.

P: The recipes that are developed in our test kitchen are commissioned by food brands who want to have their product analysed. We then create recipes to show how the product can be used differently. Our starting-point is the client's specific request. For example, there was a manufacturer of a chocolate milk drink who wanted something different from classic combinations with chocolate. The foodpairing tree showed many matches with drinks, so we thought of cocktails based on beer, tequila, calvados... Brands are often looking for another way to present their product, so we have to think outside the box a little. Recently, we made ketchup ice cream flavoured with banana, passionfruit and chocolate.

B: Foodpairing is the ideal tool to think beyond what is possible, it offers possibilities you hadn't thought of before. Many great chefs, like Sergio Herman (of Oud Sluis, The Netherlands) for example, instinctively know if a combination works but are hesitant to try it out. Customers, too, are no longer looking for jellies and foams when they go out to restaurants. They want the product as such but combined in an unexpected way. In that sense, foodpairing fits in perfectly with what chefs are looking for right now.

05 Recipes

Recipe 1

Serves 4:
2 ripe mangoes
50 ml water
a squeeze of lime juice
4 heritage tomatoes
6-8 cherry tomatoes of various colours
2 balls of buffalo mozzarella
basil leaves and slices of smoked duck breast, to garnish

Pine nut dressing:
25 g pine nuts
1 tsp aged sherry vinegar
1 tsp orange flower water
50 ml olive oil
salt and freshly ground black pepper

Tomato, mango and mozzarella salad with smoked duck and pine nut dressing

Fit the food processor with the adjustable slicing disc. Peel and slice the mangoes on the medium setting on speed 1. Place half the mango slices in a saucepan with the water. Cover the pan and cook until tender.

Slice the heritage tomatoes on the medium setting on speed 1. Place the remaining mango slices and tomatoes in a large bowl. Halve or quarter the cherry tomatoes and add to the bowl.

Fit the food processor with the mini-bowl and mini-blade. Purée the cooked mango with the lime juice on speed 2 until smooth. Leave to cool. Make the pine nut dressing. Toast the pine nuts, then process all the ingredients in the mini-bowl on speed 2 until smooth. Add a tablespoon of hot water if the dressing appears to curdle. Season to taste.

Drain the buffalo mozzarella and tear into pieces. Arrange the mango and tomato slices, cherry tomatoes and mozzarella on 4 plates. Dot with the mango purée and pine nut dressing. Garnish with basil leaves and slices of smoked duck.

A tomato is technically a fruit, so the combination with mango is not really far-fetched. The orange flower water in the vinaigrette ties it all in with the smoked duck.

RECIPE 2

Serves 4:
6-8 Grenaille potatoes
6-8 Corne de Gatte potatoes
1 large sprig of sage
2 tbsp olive oil
400 g pork fillet

Crispy shallots:
4 banana shallots
a good pinch of salt
vegetable oil, for deep-frying

Smoky vinaigrette:
100 g shallots
50 ml olive oil
1 tbsp Lapsang Souchong tea
60 ml Noilly Prat
40 ml white balsamic vinegar
100 ml sunflower oil
salt and freshly ground black pepper

Apple purée:
2 Granny Smith apples
25 g butter
1 tbsp honey

SMOKY POTATO SALAD WITH SAGE-ROAST PORK, APPLE PURÉE AND CRISPY SHALLOTS

First make the crispy shallots. Fit the food processor with the adjustable slicing disc. Peel and slice the shallots on the medium setting on speed 1. Lightly sprinkle with salt and leave for 15 minutes. Rinse the shallots, pat dry with kitchen paper and deep-fry in hot vegetable oil until golden brown and crispy. Drain on kitchen paper and leave to cool.

Wash but do not peel the potatoes, then slice on the thickest setting on speed 1. Cook the potatoes in boiling salted water until tender to the bite.

Make the smoky vinaigrette. Fit the food processor with the mini-bowl and mini-blade. Peel and finely chop the shallots on speed 1. Place in a saucepan with the olive oil and tea. Season lightly and soften for a few minutes without colouring. Add the Noilly Prat and reduce to almost nothing. Add the balsamic vinegar and reduce by two-thirds. Finally, stir in the sunflower oil and remove from the heat. Season to taste and leave to cool. When the potatoes are ready, toss with the vinaigrette and cool to room temperature.

Make the apple purée. Peel, core and roughly chop the apples. Place in a saucepan, add the butter and honey, then cook on a gentle heat until softened. Purée in the mini-bowl on speed 2 until smooth. Season to taste and keep warm.

Preheat the oven to 200°C. Crush the sage and olive oil in a pestle and mortar with a pinch of salt and pepper. Rub this mixture all over the pork. Roast in the oven for 25 to 30 minutes, then rest for 10 minutes before slicing. Serve with the smoky potato salad and apple purée. Garnish with the crispy shallots.

The smoky Lapsang Souchong enhances the nutty sweetness of the potatoes and roast pork. The apple purée balances out the dish with contrasting flavour and texture.

RECIPE 3

Serves 4:
1 large cucumber
250 g strawberries
2 handfuls of lamb's lettuce, to garnish

Mustard-honey vinaigrette:
2 tbsp wholegrain mustard
1 tbsp liquid honey
1.5 tbsp white wine vinegar
5 tbsp vegetable oil
salt and freshly ground black pepper

Gravlax tartare:
275 g gravlax (Swedish cured salmon)
finely grated zest of ½ lemon
1 tsp finely chopped chives

CUCUMBER AND STRAWBERRY CARPACCIO
WITH GRAVLAX TARTARE AND MUSTARD-HONEY VINAIGRETTE

Fit the food processor with the adjustable slicing disc. Peel the cucumber and hull the strawberries. Slice the cucumber and strawberries on the thinnest setting on speed 1. Place in a bowl and set aside.

Fit the food processor with the mini-bowl and mini-blade. Process all the ingredients for the mustard-honey vinaigrette on speed 2.

Finely chop the gravlax, then stir in the lemon zest and chives. Season to taste, then spoon on to 4 plates. Arrange the cucumber and strawberry carpaccio alongside, drizzle with the mustard-honey vinaigrette and garnish with lamb's lettuce.

Strawberry, salmon and mustard may seem an unlikely combination but honey pulls it all together by echoing the sugar in the fruit and toning down the salty flavour of the fish.

Scan the right page for 'how to make this'-instructions

RECIPE 4

Serves 4:
4 x 100 g mackerel fillets
1 tbsp olive oil
4 slices of sourdough bread
100 g cream cheese
fresh raspberries and coriander leaves, to garnish

Gin-pickled beetroot:
150 ml beetroot juice
50 ml water
50 ml white wine vinegar
50 ml gin
25 g sugar
¼ tsp coriander seeds
¼ tsp black peppercorns
1 cinnamon stick
1 star anise
125 ml olive oil
250 g raw beetroot
salt and freshly ground black pepper

MACKEREL WITH GIN-PICKLED BEETROOT ON SOURDOUGH, RASPBERRIES AND CORIANDER

First prepare the gin-pickled beetroot. Place the beetroot juice, water, vinegar, gin and sugar in a saucepan. Add the spices and bring to the boil, stirring until the sugar has dissolved. Whisk in the olive oil, season to taste and reduce to a simmer.

Fit the food processor with the adjustable slicing disc. Peel and slice the beetroot on a medium setting on speed 1. Add to the pickling liquor and cook until tender to the bite. Remove the pan from the heat and leave the beetroot to cool in the liquor. If possible, marinate overnight.

Just before serving, pan-fry the mackerel fillets in the olive oil. Spread the sourdough bread with cream cheese. Remove the beetroot slices from the pickling liquor with a slotted spoon and arrange on the bread. Place the mackerel on top and garnish with coriander leaves. Spoon some of the pickling liquor around the plate and dot with a few raspberries.

Mackerel and beetroot are a classic combo, here presented with a twist. The raspberries tie in with the sweet-and-sour beetroot, while coriander leaves provide a fresh citrus touch.

Peel 1 kg waxy potatoes, eg Grenaille. Slice the potatoes with the adjustable slicing disc on the medium setting in the work bowl on speed 1. Roughly chop 3 sprigs of tarragon, 3 sprigs of dill, a handful of chervil and ½ bunch of chives.

Place the herbs in the mini-bowl and finely chop on speed 2. Peel 2 garlic cloves, add to the mini-bowl and process again.

Melt 75 g butter, then mix into the chopped herbs on speed 1 and season. Brush an ovenproof dish with herb butter.

Arrange the potato slices in layers. Brush each layer of potatoes with herb butter, season with salt and pepper.

Bake for 1 hour in a preheated oven at 200°C until the potatoes are tender. Serve with a mixed salad and some steamed fish, if you like.

RECIPE 5

Serves 4:
25 g panko (Japanese crispy breadcrumbs)
50 g roasted peanuts
2 tbsp wholegrain mustard
4 x 100 g plaice fillets

Cauliflower:
1 cauliflower
olive oil, for roasting
2 tsp cumin seeds
grated zest of 1 lemon

Chicken jus:
300 ml good-quality chicken stock
a pinch of sugar
seeds from ½ vanilla pod
1 tbsp double cream
25 g cold butter
salt and freshly ground black pepper

PLAICE WITH MUSTARD-PEANUT CRUMBLE, CRUSHED CAULIFLOWER AND CHICKEN JUS

Preheat the oven to 200°C. Divide the cauliflower into florets and toss with a little olive oil, the cumin seeds and lemon zest. Place in a roasting tin and roast for 10 to 12 minutes until the cauliflower still retains some bite. Remove from the oven and leave to cool.

Make the chicken jus. Place the chicken stock, sugar, vanilla seeds and double cream in a saucepan and bring to the boil. Simmer until reduced by two-thirds. Whisk in the cold butter with a hand-held blender, season to taste and keep warm.

Fit the food processor with the grate/shave disc and grate the cauliflower in batches on speed 1. Tip into a bowl, season to taste and keep warm.

Fit the food processor with the mini-bowl and mini-blade. Finely chop the panko and peanuts on speed 2, then add the mustard and process on pulse until just mixed. Season to taste, then spread this mixture on to the plaice fillets. Bake in the oven for 12 to 14 minutes. Serve with the crushed cauliflower and chicken jus.

The earthy flavours of plaice and cauliflower are echoed in the peanuts, while lemon zest and mustard provide contrasting acidity. The dish is balanced out by the chicken jus.

RECIPE 6

Serves 4:
400 g celeriac
1 tbsp olive oil
4 x 125 g skinless chicken breast fillets
4 slices of Ibérico ham
100 g Manchego cheese

Orange dressing:
1 orange
1 garlic clove
50 g toasted hazelnuts
25 g flat-leaf parsley
4 tbsp olive oil
1 tbsp white balsamic vinegar
1 tbsp maple syrup
salt and freshly ground black pepper

CELERIAC REMOULADE WITH ORANGE DRESSING, MANCHEGO CHEESE AND IBÉRICO CHICKEN

First make the orange dressing. Fit the food processor with the mini-bowl and mini-blade. Remove the zest from half the orange with a vegetable peeler and place in the mini-bowl. Squeeze the juice from the orange, add to the mini-bowl with 25 g hazelnuts and the remaining ingredients. Process on speed 2 until smooth. Season to taste.

Fit the food processor with the reversible shredding disc, medium side up. Peel and shred the celeriac on speed 1. Transfer to a large bowl. Add the dressing and mix well. Cover and leave at room temperature for at least 1 hour.

Just before serving, heat the olive oil in a frying pan. Wrap the chicken fillets in the Ibérico ham slices. Season and fry until cooked all the way through. Arrange the celeriac remoulade and chicken on 4 plates. Garnish with shavings of Manchego cheese and the remaining hazelnuts. Serve with steamed new potatoes, if you like.

Nutty celeriac and hazelnuts are enriched by the Ibérico ham and Manchego cheese. The contrasting flavours of the orange vinaigrette lift the dish to a new level.

RECIPE 7

Serves 4:
4 leeks
25 g butter
100 g chorizo
½ tsp pimentón piccante (Spanish smoked paprika)
100 ml chicken stock
1 tbsp olive oil
4 x 125 g salmon fillets
75 g Gorgonzola cheese, at room temperature
salt and freshly ground black pepper

Celeriac cream:
400 g celeriac
15 g butter
150 ml whole milk

SALMON WITH CHORIZO-BRAISED LEEKS, CELERIAC CREAM AND GORGONZOLA

Fit the food processor with the adjustable slicing disc. Remove the root end and green part of the leeks and slice the rest on the thickest setting on speed 1. Melt the butter in a large pan on a medium heat. Add the leeks, season with salt and cook until softened. Finely dice the chorizo and add to the pan with the pimentón. Cook for another 5 minutes, then stir in the chicken stock. Simmer until the leeks are tender. Remove from the heat and keep warm.

Make the celeriac cream. Fit the food processor with the mini-bowl and mini-blade. Peel and roughly chop the celeriac. Melt the butter in a saucepan on a medium heat. Add the celeriac and ½ teaspoon salt. Cook for 10 minutes. Add the milk and simmer until the celeriac is tender. Tip the contents of the saucepan into the mini-bowl and purée on speed 2 until smooth. Season to taste and keep warm.

Heat the olive oil in a non-stick frying pan and fry the salmon fillets until just cooked through. Season to taste, then serve with the braised leeks and celeriac cream. Crumble the Gorgonzola around the plates and serve.

This surf 'n' turf dish pairs smoky pan-fried salmon with celeriac crème and Gorgonzola cheese. A fondue of sweet leeks with chorizo sausage balances out the dish.

RECIPE 8

Serves 4:
55 g flour
2 tbsp + 40 g sugar
1 tbsp poppy seeds
4 egg whites
½ tsp cream of tartar
a pinch of salt

Mango-coffee compote:
4 espresso coffee beans
1 ripe but firm mango
100 ml sugar syrup (made with equal
quantities sugar and water)
2 tbsp lime juice

Blueberry-lemongrass sauce:
1 lemongrass stalk
40 g sugar
1 tbsp water
100 g blueberries

ANGEL FOOD CAKES WITH MANGO-COFFEE COMPOTE AND BLUEBERRY-LEMONGRASS SAUCE

Preheat the oven to 190°C. Sift the flour and 2 tablespoons sugar into a large bowl, stir in the poppy seeds. Fit the food processor with the egg whip. Add the egg whites and cream of tartar, then whisk on speed 2 until soft peaks form. Gradually add the salt and 40 g sugar with the motor running until stiff peaks form. Gently fold into the flour. Spoon into 6 to 8 silicone muffin moulds and bake for 12 minutes until lightly golden. Leave to cool briefly, then turn out.

Prepare the mango-coffee compote. Fit the food processor with the adjustable slicing disc. Grind the coffee beans with a pestle and mortar. Peel and slice the mango on the thinnest setting on speed 1. Place the slices in a small saucepan with the coffee, sugar syrup and lime juice. Heat gently, then cover the pan and remove from the heat. Leave to infuse until ready to serve.

Make the blueberry-lemongrass sauce. Fit the food processor with the mini-bowl and mini-blade. Process the lemongrass and sugar on speed 2. Place in a small saucepan with the water and heat until the sugar has dissolved. Add the blueberries and cook until the berries have all burst. Purée the contents of saucepan in the mini-bowl on speed 2 until smooth. Leave to cool. Serve with the angel food cakes and mango compote.

Mango and blueberry is a
tried-and-tested combination but by
throwing toasty coffee and zesty
lemongrass into the mix, a whole new
dimension is created.

Scan the right page for 'how to make
this'-instructions

RECIPE 9

Serves 4:
6 g leaf gelatine
3-4 oranges
50 g sugar
½ vanilla pod
2 ripe kiwi fruit
1 tbsp acacia honey
25 g pine nuts

Goat's cheese mousse:
2 g leaf gelatine
100 ml whole milk
125 g fresh goat's cheese
2 tbsp acacia honey
2 egg whites

ORANGE-VANILLA JELLY WITH GOAT'S CHEESE MOUSSE AND KIWI PURÉE

Soak the gelatine in cold water for 10 minutes. Fit the food processor with the citrus press. Squeeze the oranges; you should obtain 250 ml of juice. Squeeze out the gelatine. Split the vanilla pod and scrape out the seeds. Gently heat a small amount of orange juice in a saucepan with the sugar, gelatine and vanilla seeds. Stir until the gelatine and sugar have dissolved, then add the remaining orange juice. Pour into a shallow tray (or into individual moulds, if you prefer) and chill until set.

Make the goat's cheese mousse. Soak the gelatine in cold water for 10 minutes. Heat the milk in a small saucepan, then squeeze out the gelatine and stir into the milk until dissolved. Process the goat's cheese in the mini-bowl on speed 2 until smooth. Add the milk mixture and acacia honey and process again. Whisk the egg whites until firm, then fold into the goat's cheese. Chill.

Peel the kiwi fruit, then purée with the acacia honey in the mini-bowl on speed 2. Toast the pine nuts in a dry pan. Slice the orange jelly into rectangles and arrange on 4 plates. Place a scoop of goat's cheese mousse alongside and finish with the kiwi purée and pine nuts.

Orange and goat's cheese is an unlikely combo but it works thanks to the honey. Its sweetness tones down the salty goat's cheese and the acidity in the fruit.

Halve 1 orange, 4 limes, 2 lemons and 1 pink grapefruit. Squeeze the fruit with the citrus press in the work bowl on speed 1. Measure 400 ml juice and pour into a saucepan with 250 g sugar. Add 600 ml sparkling wine.

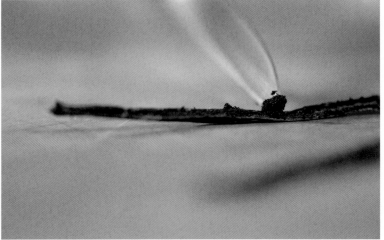

Halve 1 vanilla pod and scrape out the seeds. Add half the vanilla to the pan and bring to the boil. Pour the syrup into a shallow recipient and freeze, regularly stirring it through until the granita acquires a crystalline texture.

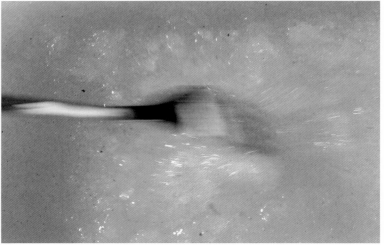

Peel 1 mango and 2 kiwi fruit. Dice with the dicing kit on speed 1.

Hull and finely chop 8 strawberries. Add 75 g blueberries and the seeds of 1/2 pomegranate.

Pour syrup into a shallow dish and freeze. Add the remaining vanilla seeds to the fruit and mix well. Serve the fruit tartare with a spoonful of granita and garnish with fresh coriander.

06 APPENDIX

NOTES FOR THE READER

1 tsp = teaspoon = 5 ml
1 tbsp = tablespoon = 15 ml
Spoon measures are always level.

1 egg = 45-50 g
1 large egg = 55-60 g

Always bring eggs to room temperature before use.
Butter is unsalted, unless stated otherwise. Double cream has a
minimum fat content of 35%. Always chill double cream before use.

Citrus fruits should be washed with warm water before grating the
zest, unless you are using unwaxed or organic fruit.
The recipes in this book were prepared in an electric oven. As all
ovens vary, use the cooking times indicated as a guideline only.
Always preheat your oven before use.

Alphabetical Index of recipes

Alphabetical Index of ingredients

CREDITS

Recipes and interviews by
Veerle de Pooter

Photography by
Tony Le Duc (recipes & product shots)
Diego Franssens (portraits)

Recipe videos by
Quality Levels Belgium
Stef Soetewey (producer/director)
Cindy Cuypers (production assistant)
Frank Dewaele (camera)
Steven Luyckfasseel (sound)
Angie Bender (chef)

Book design by
Nej De Doncker

Layout assistance by
lu'cifer

Printing and pre-press by
Symeta - Belgium
www.symeta.com

Translation by
Home Office

Printed on
Arctic Volume white, 130g/m2
(FSC labelled / environment-friendly)

Set in
Meta Pro type

© 2013

KitchenAid Europa, Inc
Nijverheidslaan 3 box 5,
B-1853 Strombeek-Bever, Belgium
www.kitchenaid.eu

EN

ISBN: 9789081634175
D/2013/11604/4

ABOUT THE AUTHORS

Veerle de Pooter (b. 1973)
was born into a family of self-taught cooks, with both her grandfather and father being enthusiastic home chefs. However, Veerle's passion for cooking was awakened while studying English away from home. After a short stint as a commis chef at a top London restaurant, Veerle returned to Belgium where she became a professional food writer and chef. In the latter capacity, she has cooked for such diverse people as a minister in the Belgian federal government, rock musicians and the acrobats of Franco Dragone's troupe.
In addition to writing regular contributions for some of the country's leading magazines, Veerle works as a translator and editor for culinary publications, such as the award-winning 'Sergiology', a limited-edition publication about top chef Sergio Herman. Veerle is author of '90 Years of KitchenAid – The Cookbook' (2009) and 'The Blender Cookbook' (2010), both published by Minestrone Cookbooks.

Tony Le Duc (b. 1961)
A father to three sons, Tony Le Duc has been a professional photographer since 1984. Often described as Flanders' most individualistic food photographer, he has illustrated more than sixty cookbooks. In 2011 FOMU (Antwerp's Photography Museum) devoted a retrospective and catalogue to Le Duc's work.
In 2004 Tony established himself as a publisher of culinary projects, creating all-in concepts in which photography, layout, typography, contents and choice of paper are all equally important. '90 Years of KitchenAid – The Cookbook' (2009), 'The Blender Cookbook' (2010) and 'Mix with the Best' (2012) have all been published by Tony Le Duc's publishing house Minestrone Cookbooks, which in 2013 was awarded 'Best Cookbook Publisher of the World' by the international 'Gourmand Cookbook Awards'.

www.minestrone.be
www.tonyleduc.eu

Nej De Doncker (b. 1958)
is a designer in the broadest sense of the word, creating graphic design for print work, as well as developing house styles and custom-built signage for buildings.
Book design is a key activity at his studio, where he develops publications for museums and artists.
In 2007 Nej co-authored the culinary publication 'Slawinski' – an homage to the controversial Belgian chef Willy Slawinski – together with Tony Le Duc. Nej was art director and designer for '90 Years of KitchenAid – The Cookbook' (2009) and 'Mix with the Best' (2012), with photography by Tony Le Duc and recipes by Sergio Herman. In 2012 he was art director and designer for the award-winning object d'art 'Sergiology', a limited-edition publication about the sources of inspiration and creations of top chef Sergio Herman.

www.nej.be